All systems go!

Leadership in a Complex World

Joe Simpson

The Leadership Centre

First published in 2014
By the Leadership Centre
Local Government House
Smith Square
London
SW1P 3HZ

www.localleadership.gov.uk

Designed and typeset by Bang Communications

ISBN 978-0-9931400-0-6

About the Author

Joe Simpson

Having read PPE at Oxford, Joe started his career in the voluntary sector, becoming Assistant Director of Community Service Volunteers. He worked in television for a number of years, heading up the ITV Telethon, working as Strategy Co-Ordinator for BBC Worldwide, and was the Director of Programmes for World Learning Network. He is also the former National Programme Director for the New Millennium Experience. In parallel, Joe spent sixteen years as a councillor in Islington. Joe's passion for and commitment to public service eventually led to him setting up the Leadership Centre in 2004. Originally Director of Politics and Partnerships, he was responsible for the pioneering Civic Pride initiative encouraging confident, capable and ambitious political leadership. As the Centre's Director, he now leads on the Leadership Centre's cross public sector programmes, working closely with senior managerial and political representatives of central and local government, health bodies, chief constables, police and crime commissioners and senior figures in the private, voluntary and third sectors.

Contents

Introduction

In 2008, I wrote a book called *The Politics of Leadership*.[1] It was an attempt to correct the comparative neglect of political leadership amidst the cascade of books and theories emerging about leadership. Indeed, such was the fashion for books on leadership that it had become 'the new black'. In addition, I wrote it in part to try and deflate some of those new orthodoxies which have emerged about how political leadership is connected with public administration. This book is not an attempt to update that argument, but to expand it into several new areas, particularly in how public services and political leadership interact with human behaviour, networks, and systems.

At the heart of the argument in *The Politics of Leadership* there were three propositions. The first was stressing the importance of storytelling, which I will return to later. The second was a reworking of the famous Mark Moore notion of the 'strategic triangle', which can be represented in two ways:[2]

Fig. 1a – Mark Moore's Strategic Triangle, as originally set out by Moore

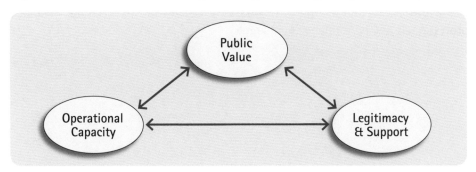

---

[1] Joe Simpson, *The Politics of Leadership: A Study of Political Leadership – Politics and Stories* (London: Leadership Centre, 2008).
[2] The strategic triangle theory was first advanced in Mark Moore, *Creating Public Value: Strategic Management in Government* (Cambridge, Massachusetts: Harvard University Press, 1997), although the strategic triangle diagrams reproduced here are not actually contained in the book itself, but are derived from Moore's subsequent presentations which summarise the book.

Fig. 1b – Mark Moore's Strategic Triangle, as amended in
The Politics of Leadership

I then described the political heartbeat, as we oscillate between the two.

Fig. 2 – The Political Heartbeat

Meanwhile, my third argument was a reworking of the existing products, professionals and performance paradigm...

Fig. 3a – Products/Professionals/Places: The old paradigm

...instead arguing for a new one about people, place and politics:

Fig. 3b – Products/Professionals/Places: a new paradigm

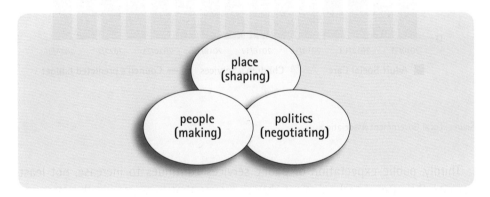

In 2008, I built on the work we had done at the Leadership Centre to help politicians rethink their roles. This book, I start from a different perspective, looking at the challenges public services face. Since 2008, we have had almost the 'perfect storm.' Public services now operate with significantly reduced budgets, and a presumption of sustained austerity. Simultaneously, there is unprecedented pressure on many public services, not least because of the rate of demographic change, best summarised in the famous 'graph of doom' which the Local Government Association produced.

Fig. 4 – The LGA's 'Graph of Doom'

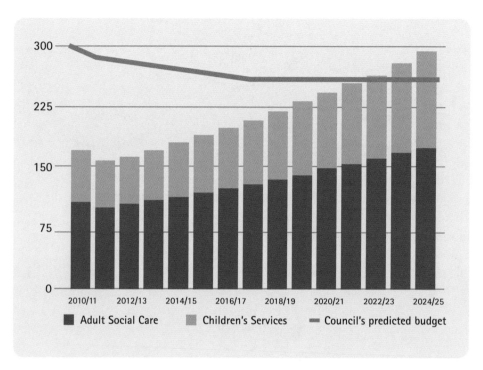

Source: Local Government Association.

Thirdly, public expectation of public services continues to increase, not least because the rate of technological change means that in so many other areas of people's lives they expect 24 7 access with immediate response.

Finally, confidence in the political process is under threat. Most British politicians thought of 2009 as the *Annus horribilis*, yet in retrospect, that was merely a point on a journey. Indeed, if we take a wider view across Western Europe, we see in many countries a significant decline in support for mainstream parties, and the rise of more radical voices. The continuing mix of economic stagnation, and the increased pace of change in other areas such as emigration, has created new challenges for politicians as they seek to engage citizens.

In the same way that politicians need to rethink their role, so we need to consider how we do public services. The existing mantras of 'New Public Management' (NPM) and their like are just not fit for purpose in this new world. Instead I argue for a more systemic framing. The phrase 'systems leadership' has acquired some traction in recent years. At the Leadership Centre, we have played our part in promoting approaches based on it; yet I think the language itself needs to evolve. It fails what the Americans call 'the elevator pitch concept' (can you summarise your idea before – in our idiom – the lift reaches the floor of the person to whom we are pitching).

Parallel to the NPM mindset is the often-default position of 'If it's difficult, let's do a restructuring, and that will solve our problems.' This continues to be repeated despite the cumulative evidence that it does not work. I think the best summary of why that is the case comes from Peter Smith, the CEO of Adelaide Council in Australia. Speaking to the Australian Local Leadership Conference in 2014, with the earthiness only an Australian would use on a public platform, he described this approach as 'frigging with the rigging.'

Instead I try and describe what a systems approach would look and feel like. In advocating this, I am not suggesting that traditional management approaches should all be abandoned. Instead, to use the heartbeat analogy again, leaders need to be able to switch between traditional management practices, and more systemic approaches. Given the challenges we face, that heartbeat is now faster, so it is even more vital that public sector leaders can adapt to that rhythm. This book is meant as an aide to that adaptation.

CHAPTER ONE

Leadership of Place

In *The Politics of Place*, I developed an argument about the key skills needed for 'place shaping' - that leadership of place role that is now at the core of what local government does.[3] I argued there were ten key challenges as follows:

1. **Steering not rowing.** Since the publication of *Reinventing Government* over a decade ago, there has been increasing recognition of the need for public leaders to focus more on steering rather than rowing. If we look at the range of areas we have identified for attention by local government it would simply be impossible for local government to directly run all those services and also maintain the ability to be proactive and strategic.

2. **Commissioning and co-commissioning.** It is not sufficient to have the vision; councils need to be better at commissioning - in other words, they have to be able to articulate clearly the outcomes they are seeking. Moreover, much of this commissioning will need to be done in consultation with other partners. These commissioning skills (quite different from pure procurement ones) are strategic and need to be developed at the most senior level.

---

[3] Joe Simpson, *The Politics of Place* (London: Leadership Centre, 2006).

3. **Influence, not command and control.** As the democratically-elected body, the authority has significant moral influence and authority. Yet that does not translate into direct control. For example, local authorities cannot force private businesses to invest in their town, as opposed to elsewhere, perhaps even another country.

4. **Convening (and being convened).** Authorities have a critical role in convening others; in other words, creating common agendas where all partners can see the benefit in collaboration. This requires the ability to see, identify and communicate the longer-term desired outcome. But this also requires developing the flexibility to understand other agendas and problem-solving techniques that buy stakeholders into shared solutions rather than separate ones.

5. **Thinking and acting long term.** Authorities have to be the champions of longer-term vision. Clarity of purpose and vision, and the stability (and predictability) that should flow from that, are all critical to creating the climate of confidence that can secure the participation of others.

6. **Coping with complexity.** Partnership-working is messy and complex. In this world of place shaping there will be very many partners, working in many different partnerships and working to very different timescales. Authorities have to develop the maturity and the confidence to operate in this more complex world.

7. **Listening and engaging.** If local authorities are to succeed with this agenda, it is not enough for there to be great plans; local people must have a sense of ownership, and stakeholders must believe they have a real opportunity to influence and design outcomes. In other words, listening and engaging skills are critical. We have seen the consequences of top-down major development; the lesson to learn is not that there has been any inappropriateness in terms of "masterplanning", but more that the problem lies in only engaging the expert! Engagement is not just about ownership, it involves people doing things. A devolutionary agenda only has meaning if there are active citizens prepared and supported to engage. Within this world, the sort of performance indicator needed would evaluate the level of increased citizen engagement in making their place better.

8. **Community mediation.** Any change involves difficult decisions. A unique role of the politician is to help people understand issues, and to help find solutions that can get buy-in from local residents - who in turn may not have got what they wanted, but can at least understand why certain decisions were made. More generally, the greater the scale of change, the more important the need for the mediation to provide the glue to help places hold together.

9. **Storytelling.** Shaping places means changing places, sometimes physically, sometimes more ephemerally, but it involves being able to picture (or more often part-picture) those changes. It's the quality of the story that determines the success or otherwise of the enterprise. We know that the change we have seen in many of our great cities in the last couple of decades is the direct result of local leaders with the clarity of story to see a different future for their place. Such aspirations need articulating: therefore the role of storytelling becomes a key political attribute, for the story has to have the power to bind together citizens and stakeholders in the pursuit of a common goal. Thus it is not purely one person's story (or even one authority's story). This organic role of storytelling naturally evolves as time goes on and people's lives are affected by it.

10. **Strategic and community leadership.** Vision alone is not sufficient. What matters is the ability to mobilise others to make things happen. The attributes referred to above all culminate in the strategic leadership skills required to create and sustain the coalitions required to make leadership of place possible. But this has to happen at both the wider strategic level, and at the very local neighbourhood level. The language of "frontline councillors" is now well established. But we should not see that role as exclusively one for non-executive councillors. All councillors need to be able to champion the neighbourhoods in the ward they represent.

CHAPTER TWO

Politics and Civil Society

At the beginning of his premiership, David Cameron made it clear that his commitment to the Big Society agenda should be one of the defining features of his premiership. As time passed (and particularly after his key adviser Steve Hilton emigrated to California), use of the phrase was reduced. What has been interesting is the response to this aspiration. There are critics from the left who see his aspirations as a fig-leaf for radical cuts. But equally, there have been others who have argued that it would be a tremendous mistake to so dismiss this (even if they would use different language to describe the opportunity). Meanwhile, there have been many prominent Conservatives who are thought to be very sceptical. The 'Big Society' was never part of the George Osborne lexicon; whilst Andy Coulson, the erstwhile director of communications at No 10 was clearly sceptical, if not downright opposed (and his successor Craig Oliver even more so).

The purpose here is to put this agenda within a wider context, and to explore why this issue – far from being one which divides purely on a party basis – seems instead to show differences within parties. All political parties are coalitions. I do not accept that the language of left and right is now superfluous. Of course politicians have to fight over the centre ground, but leaving aside the clear differences between those on the right wing of the Conservative Party and those on the left wing of the Labour Party, anyone meeting groups of political activists within the three parties would recognise different centres of gravity for each. But whilst there is a left/right axis, there are also different perspectives which see other areas of difference. This agenda is an illustration of one such issue.

The Big Society and the Conservative Tradition

Many commentators have pointed out that the Cameron project has strong historic roots in the Conservative party tradition.[4] Most famously, this is a reworking of the Burkean cry in favour of "little platoons". Edmund Burke was an MP from 1766 to 1794. He was a prominent writer on political themes for over 40 years. He is perhaps now most famous for two things. First his passionate defence of MPs as representatives and not delegates.

Parliament is not a congress of ambassadors from different hostile interests, which interests must maintain, as an agent and advocate, against other agents and advocates. Instead, Parliament is a deliberative assembly of one nation, with one interest, that of the whole; where the general good should guide, resulting from the general reason of the whole - not local purposes, nor local prejudices. You do indeed choose a member to represent you; but when you have chosen him or her, they are not a member of Bristol, but a Member of Parliament.

Secondly, in 1790 Burke wrote his *Reflections on the Revolution in France*.[5] Burke was a Whig, and has been claimed at different times as an advocate for both liberal sentiments and conservative ones. *Reflections* came towards the end of his life, and sounded clear warnings about the speed of change in the French Revolution. Rather than seeing this as the transition from liberal to conservative, I think there is more consistency in Burke's thinking, which appears most clearly in his argument about society. David Cameron's take on this is best summarised in his line 'There is such a thing as society, it's just not the same thing as the state.'[6] This formulation was meant to distinguish himself from the oft-quoted line of Margaret Thatcher about there being no such thing as society. In fact if we read that quote in context there is not such a difference. It reads

> There is no such thing as society. There is living tapestry of men and women and people and the beauty of that tapestry and the quality of our lives will depend upon how much each of us is prepared to take responsibility for ourselves and each of us is prepared to turn round and help by our own efforts those who are unfortunate.[7]

---

[4] See, for instance, Matthew Parris, 'Return of the Top Toff', *The Times*, October 20, 2005, p. 20.

[5] Edmund Burke, *Reflections on the Revolution in France* (London: SMK Books, 2012 [first pub. 1790]).

[6] David Cameron victory speech after Conservative leadership contest, *BBC News*, December 6, 2005, http://news.bbc.co.uk/1/hi/uk_politics/4504722.stm .

[7] Margaret Thatcher interview, *Woman's Own*, September 23, 1987, reproduced by Margaret Thatcher Foundation, http://www.margaretthatcher.org/document/106689

Back to Burke, the text of his 'little platoons' argument in *Reflections* reads as follows:

> To be attached to the subdivision, to love the little platoon we belong to in society, is the first principle (the germ as it were) of public affections. It is the first link in the series by which we proceed toward a love to our country and to mankind. The interest of that portion of social arrangement is a trust in the hands of all those who compose it; and as none but bad men would justify it in abuse, none but traitors would barter it away for their own personal advantage.[8]

You can see in this the consistency of a key strand of conservative thought, with its stress on context and tradition shaping what is possible. Conservative critics often portray the Conservatives as an anti-thinking party. However, the Burke argument (picked up by Michael Oakeshott amongst others) expresses scepticism about having an overreliance on rationalism.[9] In more modern terms about government, this would translate as a presumption against assuming that comprehensive bureaucratic solutions actually work. Karl Popper called for "piecemeal social engineering".[10] Popper's argument about science was that it was based on trial and error. Similarly, he was pro-piecemeal social engineering rather than holistic experiments. With this approach, conservatism is not so much against change, but is risk-averse, and desires incremental change based on rigorous evidence.

Burke believed in an organic society, and he believed that as individuals we would best flourish within such a society. He was thus an early champion of what would later come to be called 'One Nation' conservatism. However, there are other major strands of conservative thinking. If Burke can be seen as representing a more optimistic vision of mankind, there have been others with more pessimistic assumptions. Historically, you could call this the 'original sin' thesis. With this perspective you are more sceptical about our natural aspirations to do good. One key British thinker in this tradition was Thomas Hobbes. For him, man is 'continually in competition for honour and dignity...and consequently amongst men there ariseth on that ground, envy and hatred, and finally war.'[11] His *Leviathan* became an

---

[8] Edmund Burke, *Reflections on the Revolution in France* (London: SMK Books, 2012 [first pub. 1790]).
[9] See, for instance, Michael Oakeshott, *Rationalism in Politics, and Other Essays* (Indianapolis, Indiana: Liberty Press, 1991).
[10] Karl Popper, *The Poverty of Historicism* (London: Routledge and Kegan Paul, 1961 [rev. ed.]), p. 43.
[11] Thomas Hobbes, *Leviathan, Parts I and II* (Plymouth: Broadway Press, 2005 [first pub. 1651]), p.127.

argument about the need for a strong, indeed absolutist, state. His solution is not one many would now advocate – but the argument still resonates, if with a different tone. A different tone would refer to the need for a more muscular state, committed to enforcing rules. Calls for 'law and order', and a strong national defence, would be the hallmarks of this in modern conservatism.

The late Sir Simon Milton Milton – a highly influential Deputy Mayor of London, and long-serving Leader of Westminster City Council – referred to himself as a Peelite. Sir Robert Peel is still best known for his role in establishing a police force during his spell as Home Secretary. Peel's most well-known phrase is perhaps 'the police are the public, and the public are the police.'[12] His 'Tamworth Manifesto' should be regarded as the launch pad of the Conservative Party as we know it, enshrining the principle that the party would 'reform to survive.' For Simon Milton, what Peel was addressing was the need to create a framework of enforceable rules about the conditions in which we coexist in modern urban society.

In the last century, the third key leg of conservative thinking has been the defence of the free market. That approach was originally perhaps best articulated by Adam Smith. Smith saw himself as much as a political philosopher as an economist who (like Burke) could also be claimed within a liberal tradition. Indeed for much of the time economic liberalism was not a cornerstone of conservatism (which had more sympathy with arguments about protectionism). But the great attribute of Conservative Party's thinking is that, whilst it retains its scepticism to rationalist approaches to change, once change happens, it recalibrates itself to adopt new positions. So by the mid-twentieth century, economic liberalism had become a core conservative belief. In advocating the efficiency of the market, Smith had no illusions about the aspirations of businesses (as suppliers to be monopolists, or as purchasers to operate within a free market). For Smith the 'invisible hand' delivered the outcome despite the best intentions of the players to distort the outcome. The brilliance of the Smith argument was that whilst accepting Hobbesian scepticism, he proposed a solution to get what he believed would be the most desirable outcome for all.

These perspectives are not in total opposition to each other. And individual Conservatives will often advocate all three. But if we think of differing primary perspectives you can see how David Cameron, postulating an optimistic view of mankind, and armed with an argument about nudge theory to further encourage

---

[12] Sir Robert Peel, 'Principles of Law Enforcement, 1829', reproduced on the Durham Constabulary website, www.durham.police. ac.uk/About-Us/Documents/Peels_Principles_Of_Law_Enforcement.pdf

action does believe that people would be willing to do more to engage with fellow citizens. Meanwhile other Conservatives with other primary perspectives would be more sceptical.

Alongside David Cameron in this advocacy has been Philip Blond. His 'Red Tory' brand has let tp considerable press interest, and his brand has also attracted its Labour mirror image to adopt a similar language (See 'Blue Labour' below).[13] But I do not sense that Blond has himself moved the centre of gravity of Conservative thinking on this agenda. Nor is it a prerequisite of advocating the 'Big Society' to also advocate the wider Blond thesis. I would describe Blond as extending that agenda, not underpinning it.

The Good Society and the Labour Tradition

The 'Good Society' is the language used initially by David Millband and then subsequently also by his brother Ed.[14] It has an obvious resonance with the "Great Society" phrase used by Lyndon B. Johnson ("LBJ") when he was President of the United States. In using this language, Labour was asserting its claim to ownership of this strain of thinking. Through most of the nineteenth century, much left-of-centre and radical thinking was highly sceptical about the role of the state. Indeed, set against a backdrop where state intervention had traditionally meant oppression of the people, from the Cavalier cause of the English Civil War to the Peterloo Massacre of 1819, the aspiration was to remove many of the impositions of the state on people's lives. So through the nineteenth century we saw the evolution of strong forms of association, independent of the state: co-operatives, mutuals (local building societies and savings organisations), and also trade unions. There were also federal support organisations. The TUC is the *Trades* Union Congress. It is only recently that we have seen the emergence of the small number of large multi-purpose organisations we have today. Instead, the original building block was around association and shared common interest of specific groups of workers.

Not everyone on the left was so equivocal about the state. Much of Marxism was more focused on the role of the state – and the way in which European Communist parties evolved was around a clear focus on securing (and then ruthlessly using) levers of power. But as Tony Benn was fond of saying, the Labour

---

[13] See Philip Blond, Red Tory: *How Left and Right Have Broken Britain and How We Can Fix It* (London: Faber & Faber, 2010).
[14] Allegra Stratton and Patrick Wintour, 'David Miliband's Leadership Speech That Only His Wife Heard', *The Guardian*, June 10, 2010, p. 4; Allegra Stratton, 'Ed Miliband Rehearses "Good Society" Guru's Lines in Conference Speech', *The Guardian*, September 28, 2010, p. 6.

movement in Britain owed more to Methodism than to Marxism. Indeed, Methodism could itself be described as a form of civic movement.

The drive within the Labour tradition for an interventionist state came not from Marxism, but a very different perspective: the Fabian tradition. The early Fabians were more middle class intellectuals, most famously epitomised by Sydney and Beatrice Webb. The Webbs were, for a time, seduced by the appearances of change in Russia, but this was not from any connection of them to radical left thinking-rather they were seduced by the stories of directed change which they heard on their travels. This tradition- perhaps best remembered in the immortal phrase "the man in Whitehall knows best", believed in the rational, intelligent planning of the world of bureaucracy (and the parallel belief that as the most rational and intelligent they would be best suited to lead such bureaucracies).

The phrase itself is remembered but was not always used in the way we now remember it. In his book *The Socialist Case*, what Douglas Jay said was 'in the case of nutrition and health, just as in the case of education, the gentleman in Whitehall really does know better what is good for people than the people know themselves.'[15] Jay may have wanted to imply this as exception, rather than a general rule, but Jay epitomised this strand of thinking.

But Labour's conversion to the cause of rational planning (in modern parlance, the world of 'top-down targets', and 'evidence-based policy') was not a guaranteed outcome. The nineteenth century mutualist tradition continued into the twentieth century. Indeed, the Co-operative movement sought political representation, in 1920 establishing the Co-operative Party as a sister party to the Labour Party. (The founding General Secretary was one Samuel Perry, who later became an MP. As an aside, Perry is less remembered now for those roles, but as the father of Fred Perry the tennis player). In terms of the battle of ideas, however, perhaps the most significant thinker was G.D.H. Cole, and his advocacy of 'Guild Socialism', though other colleagues such as Harold Laski also played their role.[16]

As a headline summary you could say Webb 3, Cole 1 – with victory coming to the Webb team with two late goals. Marc Stears is an Oxford politics don, who is very close to Ed Milliband, and is one of the thinkers associated with Blue Labour thinking. He has written about the twists and turns of this debate, and how it played on each side of the Atlantic. In one of the ironies of political evolution, the American left had originally been much more attracted to what Stears calls

---

[15] Douglas Jay, *The Socialist Case* (London: Faber & Faber 1937), p. 317.
[16] See G.D.H. Cole, *Guild Socialism Re-Stated* (London: Leonard Parsons, 1920).

'progressive nationalism' – originally championed by Theodore Roosevelt in his unsuccessful 1912 run to return as President. Roosevelt lost out to Woodrow Wilson, who subsequently also secured re-election in 1916. But with America's involvement in the World War, and Wilson's ill-health, there was an increasing authoritarian streak to the administration. American progressives had been initially attracted to the nationalist strand because of the weaknesses they perceived in the American tradition of town hall democracy, but this switch in tone by the Wilson administration led them to explore for a while something much closer to the 'guild socialism' tradition. Stears points to the two way travel of people and thinking (Laski for instance left England in 1916, first to McGill, and then to Harvard).

In Britain, war had a different effect on Labour thinking. The planning/pluralist debate continued within the Labour tradition through the 1920s and 1930s; but by the end of this period, the working assumption throughout the Second World War had been about the importance of state planning.[17] Labour had of course been part of the Government, and Labour Ministers had personal experience of undertaking such roles, particularly in administering 'the Home Front'. So once in power with a majority government after the war, the decisions about how to implement change continued in that tradition. There were two key illustrations which show that change. The first was Bevan's decision to go for a **national** health service. Labours commitment to a radical change in the health service, with universal access was never in doubt, and the phrase 'National Health Service' did appear in the 1945 Labour manifesto, but its meaning was far from clear – there was no guaranteed presumption that the only way to do this was through one National Health Service, rather than more universal provision of local health services. The second was the creation of the National Coal Board. Again, whether there would be radical change was not the question. But whether there would be more worker control, or a more traditional company structure, was the main question. It was the latter which seemed the much less risky option.

Since then, the default position of post-war Labour thinking has normally been to presume some 'national planning' approach, and that evolved under Blair away from a planning culture to a targets one; but again, it was driven by a fairly centralised agenda. It was only towards the end of the Blair regime that there were the beginnings of the first shoots of what might have been a more localist, pluralist spring.

---

[17] See the central argument of Paul Addison, T*he Road to 1945: British Politics and the Second World War* (London: Jonathan Cape, 1975).

Maurice Glasman, a Labour peer ennobled by Ed Milliband, is the author of the phrase 'Blue Labour'.[18] Glasman was certainly a key advocate of a more co-operative, localist thinking strand within Labour. For a while he had the ear of the Leader, but more lastingly, Jon Cruddas was a key supporter. With Cruddas appointed to chair the Labour policy review, this more decentralised agenda started to get traction. In parallel, the Co-operative Councils Innovation Network was established.[19] Originally chaired by Steve Reed (now an MP, but then the Leader of Lambeth Council) and subsequently by Jim McMahon (Leader of Oldham Council and since then also Leader of the Labour group at the Local Government Association), so creating a more 'bottom-up' momentum.

In parallel, we should also note the championship of 'Movement for Change' by David Miliband (a move subsequently supported by his brother) - which sought to mobilise 10,000 community organisers as a way of re-connecting the Labour Party with local residents. This built on Saul Alinsky's social movement techniques developed in the States.[20]

Community Politics and the Liberal Democrat Tradition

Distinguishing between state and society has of course been a hallmark of liberal thinking for centuries. As the party of John Stuart Mill, many Liberal Democrats would claim this almost as a birth right, although even within the old Liberal Party there still remained some tension, with many of the "Progressive Liberals" of the Liberal Party at its zenith becoming advocates of an interventionist state. However, there may be more value in considering this debate within more recent history. After the Second World War, the then-Liberal Party was almost annihilated. 1951 saw the high point of two-party politics, (the Liberals winning only a 2.5 % share of the vote). The Liberals were reduced to six seats that were either in the Celtic fringes, or resulted from local electoral pacts with Conservatives. The arrival of Jo Grimond as Leader in 1956 led to some revival (and the famous win by Eric Lubbock in the Orpington by election in 1962). Though not triggering any radical trajectory of new seats, there was the emergence of a radical Young Liberal wing, the party's so-called 'Red Guard'.[21]

---

[18] For a further elaboration on this, see Maurice Glasman, 'Blue Labour and Labour History', Labour History Research Unit, Anglia Ruskin University (October, 2012).

[19] Sarah Marsh, 'What We've Learned: The Co-operative Councils Innovation Network', *Guardian*, July 9, 2013, p. 7.

[20] See Saul Alinsky, *Rules for Radicals* (New York: Random House, 1971).

[21] Peter Hellyer, 'Young Liberals: The "Red Guard" Era', *Journal of Liberal Democrat History*, 17 (Winter 1997-8), pp. 13-5.

A brilliant publication by David Boyle, *Communities Actually*, tells the story.[22] The debate the Young Liberals had was about what would be their distinctive approach. Starting in 1969-70 this evolved as 'Community Politics'. A key group of people were responsible for that thinking. One was Tony (now Lord) Greaves, who has remained a full-time local Liberal Democrat campaigner in Pendle. A second, Peter Hain, argued for more of a 'direct action' focus, and subsequently became a Labour Minister. But two others (the original authors of the phrase "community politics") went on to other claims to fame. Gordon Lishman subsequently became Chief Executive of Age Concern, whilst (Professor Sir) Lawrence Freedman became, perhaps, Britain's most significant defence and foreign policy analyst of the late twentieth century.

The 'community politics' arguments they espoused argued for a different way of doing things, and became the platform for the re-emergence of the then-Liberal Party into urban (or more frequently, suburban) England. As now practised, this approach attracts shared hostility from both Labour and Conservative opponents. (There is a shared joke which Conservative and Labour candidates tell. Your two opponents are standing by the edge of a deep cliff. You have the opportunity to push one – but only one – off the cliff; which one do you choose? The answer is (depending on whether you are Labour or Conservative) Conservative or Labour, with the punch line 'business before pleasure'. It certainly is the case that, in many local Lib Dem campaigns, the mantras continue (six Focus leaflets, five attack messages, and one positive message at the end, plus the inevitable 'It's a two-horse race' with the Lib Dems just behind in second place, so if you want to stop X winning, you must vote LibDem). However if you go to the origins of the approach, there was no presumption of electoral success. As Bernard Greaves and Gordon Lishman's influential *The Theory and Practice of Community Politics* makes clear in its opening sentence, 'Community politics is not a technique for the winning of local government elections.'[23] It was an argument about a different way of engaging with people, in the hope that it would also pay electoral dividends.

But even within Liberal Democrats, there remain fault lines. Originally these tensions could be seen between what was perceived as a radical and urbanised

---

[22] David Boyle, *Communities Actually: A Study of Liberal Democrat Localism in Action* (London: LGA Liberal Democrats, 2007). See also Peter Hain (ed.), *Community Politics* (London: John Calder, 1976), and John Meadowcroft, 'Community Politics: A Study of the Liberal Democrats in Local Government' (Goldsmith's College, University of London, Ph.D., 1999).

[23] Bernard Greaves and Gordon Lishman, *The Theory and Practice of Community Politics: ALC Booklet #12* (Hebden Bridge: Association of Liberal Councillors, 1980).

youth wing, and a more traditional Liberal wing with much more profound scepticism about any type of collective intervention. The emergence of the SDP is often described as a left/right fissure within the Labour Party. There was also the fault line about Europe. But culturally, the bulk of the SDP cohort were classic Fabianistas (who even set up their own version of the Fabian Society, the Tawney Society, after they found themselves barred from Fabian meetings). The one prominent defector who did not join the newly-merged party was David Owen, who was also the one SDP member with the least affinity with that strand of thinking, and his own political trajectory emphasising a 'social market economy' led Owen to endorse the Conservatives in 1992, and for prominent Owenites such as Danny Finkelstein to join the Conservatives. (There was also one prominent Liberal who for a long time refused to join the newly-merged party, Michael Meadowcroft, who had been MP for Leeds West. Meadowcroft's critique was that the merged party was too centrist in thinking.)[24]

As a more light-hearted summary of this tension, here is Baroness Ros Scott, on what she learned from her time as President of the Liberal Democrats:

> that the new party had combined the two key attributes of the two old parties, from the Liberals a default mistrust of the leadership by the activists, and from the SDP a default mistrust of the activists by the leadership.[25]

Summary

This question of politics and civil society is one which permeates the traditions of all three parties. In each, it is not unproblematic. And whilst some of the manifestations of this thinking could be seen as shared, it is important to understand how these approaches have different manifestations - and very different languages – in the different party traditions.

So rather than see the 'Big Society' as an apolitical idea, it is better to think of it as a shaping question. The different political answers to this question reflect the different traditions and aspirations of parties.

Furthermore, if these approaches are to have real meaning, rather than merely be gestures, then we must recognise that the organisational is also political. The way of promoting things to be done, or the way of doing things, manifests itself in different political approaches.

---

[24] Michael Meadowcroft, *Focus on Freedom: The Case for the Liberal Party* (Southport: Liberal Party, 1992 [rev. 3rd ed., 2001]).
[25] Private information.

CHAPTER THREE

Civil Society

What constitutes the personal can change over time. One way of summarising much of post-war social legislation has been to remove the state from regulating different spaces, e.g. more liberal divorce rules, removing statutory barriers to gay and lesbian rights, etc. The recent debate about the rights and wrongs of super injunctions is again about what should be the limits of privacy. But whilst this boundary moves over time, (and between cultures) there still is a boundary.

The boundary between what is family and what is social is porous. An Irish way of describing where you are from is to say 'My people are from...', so we can have notions of extended families or clans which themselves would be more appropriately seen as within civil society.

Equally, whilst it is true that 'there is such a thing as society, it's just different to the state', we can also see that boundary as porous. Let me give two examples of organisations that we would see as key parts of civil society: the WRVS and Citizens Advice.

The WRVS (now the Royal Voluntary Service) was formed in 1938, originally as the Women's Voluntary Services for Defence. The proposal for the initiative came from the then Home Secretary, Sir Samuel Hoare, who wrote to the Marchioness of Reading. Her response was important. She wrote:

> This work is done in alliance with the Home Office and not merely as part of your departmental organisation. I think you will agree if we succeed in

enrolling women we will be...more successful as an outside body working <u>with</u> you than as officers.

In that analysis, she was certainly proved right. By 1943 there were one million volunteers.

Discussions about the need for better advice to citizens had been a feature of discussions for some time. The then-National Council of Social Service (the precursor of today's National Council for Voluntary Organisations) was critical to this. But the instigator for action was World War Two. War was declared on September 3, 1939. By September 4, two hundred bureaus had already been opened.

But whilst there is some blurring between civil society and the state, they are not contiguous. We can put this more strongly: a key attribute of absolutist or totalitarian regimes is their inevitable desire to rein in the civic sphere, and to turn it into an arm of government.

Civic association is in the main a freely organised act, and not part of any central plan. (Michael Oakeshott made the contrast between civic association and enterprise association, the latter having a more directing purpose. The risk with the latter is the tendency to drift towards an imposed direction). To illustrate the self-directed (as opposed to other-directed) nature of civic association, the Countryside Alliance and the League Against Cruel Sports are both examples of civic association – but their aspirations are certainly not aligned. Another way to demonstrate this diversity is to consider the experience of virtually everyone who becomes a civic Mayor. Election to this post tends to be a recognition of long service, rather than as a trajectory to higher posts. People who become Mayors therefore tend to have a long cumulative history of involvement in the place they represent. Yet talk to any Mayor after their year in office, and they nearly always say they just did not realise the diversity of civic life in their borough or town, and that is because so little of what constitutes the civic sphere is in any way aligned to the activities of local (or national) government. Of course, some parts of the civil sphere are more aligned with government; many disability charities, for instance, are now also delivery arms for government.

Secondly, civic associations are partial. You tend to favour members of your association against others. For instance, if you are a member of a local resident's society you are promoting the interests of local residents (or what you perceive to be their interests). This can be a question not merely of partiality, but also judgement. If you are a member of any of the major faith groups, part of your belief system is that you are a believer as opposed to others, who are either non-believers, or else believe in the different things. (Jeffrey Alexander refers to the 'civil sphere' to describe the space where civic action takes place.)[26]

Jeffrey Alexander refers to the "civil sphere" to describe the space where civic action takes place. He acknowledges the value ('Civil solidarity is a big tent'). But also recognises that "the discourse of civil society is divided into either/or binaries". He echoes the words of one the founding fathers of social anthropology, Evans-Pritchard, who wrote "A man sees himself as a member of a group only in opposition to other groups". This binary tension Alexander explores to better understand the political process. But it also has meaning when we talk about building community organisations. Here is a much younger Barack Obama (1988) reflecting on his years of community organising in Chicago "we tend to think of organising as a mechanical, instrumental thing" instead he argues it is really about "building a culture" which means "building up stories and getting people to reflect on what their lives mean and how people in the neighbourhood can be heroes, and how they are part of a larger force".

The 2008 Barack Obama operation was community organising, writ large. So here was the Camp Obama mantra:

IS	IS NOT
Story	Task
Mutual	Interview
Conversation	Prying
Curiosity	Fact
Why, How	What
Specific	Abstract

The second half of the pitch shows what happens when people are organised:

BREAKING THE BELIEF BARRIER

Fear	⟶	Hope
Apathy	⟶	Anger
Inertia	⟶	Urgency
Isolation	⟶	Solidarity

[26] See Jeffrey C. Alexander, *The Civil Sphere* (Oxford: Oxford University Press, 2006).

Another way of looking at this is through the approach of Robert Putnam. His most famous work is *Bowling Alone*.[27] Putnam uses the example of ten-pin bowling to highlight his key concern. Noting that whilst bowling continues to be popular, there has been a radical decline in bowling leagues, Putnam uses this as a metaphor for the decline in social capital in America (what we might call the output of civil society).

Putnam also makes a contrast between what he calls 'bridging' and 'bonding' capital. Bridging capital would connect people not already connected. (Major national events such as the recent Royal wedding would be an illustration of something which creates this.) Bonding capital reinforces connections between people already connected (a school re-union would be an illustration of this). Advocates of international sport often argue that international competitions foster bridging capital, connecting people who would not otherwise connect or understand each other. Sometimes, that is the case – but a Rangers v Celtic football match basically demonstrates the potential downside of 'bonding capital', as we get the reinforcement of almost tribal groupings.

Similarly, advocates of social media argue that it connects people who would not otherwise know each other (or at least, would not know each other as well) – though more detailed analyses often show that social media in fact connects similar people, with similar world views, providing something of an 'echo chamber' effect. A classic illustration of the 'echo chamber' effect, from before the age of social media, came when journalist Pauline Kael achieved notoriety after Richard Nixon's landslide 1972 election victory. A metropolitan New Yorker who had proudly voted for the arch-liberal George McGovern, she wrote 'I live in a rather special world. I only know of one person who voted for Nixon. Where they are I don't know. They're outside my ken. But sometimes when I'm in a theatre I can feel them.'[28] Kael was widely ridiculed because she could not believe, based on the views of her own social circle, that there was a majority out there that was willing to vote for Nixon. The advent of social media, bonding people to like-minded peers, has acted as a multiplier of this effect.

Our aspiration should therefore be for a society rich in both building and bonding capital. We should also try and understand what actions might stimulate both. So what might be the prompts for me to engage in the civil sphere? When we go on

---

[27] See Robert D. Putnam, *Bowling Alone: The Collapse and Revival of American Community* (New York: Simon & Schuster, 2000), esp. pp. 111-5.
[28] Pauline Kael, *The New Yorker*, December 28, 1972.

holiday, most of us aim to act responsibly. We might even like the people and place we visit so much that we might think of relocating there; but we do not see ourselves as citizens of that place (unless we have actually relocated). We would accept some basic rules (of the 'When in Rome, do as the Romans do' variety), but we do not see ourselves as civil actors. Of course there could be times when we get "caught up in things", such as a major disaster where we would engage with fellow citizens because of the scale of the emergency, but that would be the exception, not the rule. Similarly, if you look at places with large student populations, large numbers of students do not engage in any non-university related activity, seeing themselves as temporary residents.

It is not just perceived 'temporary association' that might be the reason for non-engagement. Consider voting – an illustration of civic engagement. There has been a lot of concern about declining engagement by younger people. This could indicate a long-term cyclical decline of interest in politics; but an equally plausible explanation would be the delay in people getting married, or having children. Birth rates are actually rising again, but the average age for women giving birth has gone up. In Britain, the average age of a first-time mother is now 31. Having children connects you more to local life (from the hospital visits, or the local doctor, to being the mum or dad at the school gate). Two key attributes therefore are locality, and purpose or interest. In this sense, talk of "Big Society" might get us off on the wrong track – we might more usefully talk about strong local society, or local society as the building block of a "Big Society." A third attribute has to be opportunity. That is twofold: on the supply side, we have more or less scope to do things at different points in our lives. One of Putnam's key maxims is how small increases in commuting times lead to big decreases in the amount of social capital generated, so where we live and work can also affect this. But on the demand side, we know that there are differences. So towns that are in effect modern commuter dormitories face different challenges to say an historic city, with a legacy of civic engagement.

Understanding the importance of locality (and a sense of locality) in creating civil society might also help us understand why it has proved difficult for national politicians to drive this agenda. David Cameron has tried to ignite Big Society on a number of occasions- but the national reception has been lukewarm. He is not the first national politician to try this. David Ennals, as Secretary of State for the then Department of Health and Social Security in the late 1970s, tried to mobilise a 'Good Neighbour' campaign. Douglas Hurd, as Home Secretary, tried to talk up the idea of 'Active Citizenship'. Margaret Thatcher launched 'UK 2000', with Richard

Branson as Chairman. None of these initiatives really got traction – all received criticism for being launched at a time of fiscal retrenchment. However, for me the weakness in all these initiatives was not the question of finance, but their inability to be grounded in people's actual lives in real communities. In other words, there was a disconnect between the (national) idea and the (local) delivery.

A second difficulty for these approaches has been the presumption that these should be almost anti-political, as if politics and civil society are at odds. Contrary to that view, we need to recognise that an active political process is a key test of successful civil society. It is quite common for people to observe that organisations such as the Royal Society for the Protection of Birds have many more members than our main political parties do. It is also the case that across the western world, political party membership has been in decline for some time.

However, as Gerry Stoker has argued, if you ask 'how many people are active as volunteers in these other organisations?', or indeed 'how active are members in deciding what policies these organisations pursue?', we would get a very different answer. It remains the case that the political parties are essentially organisations built and sustained by the voluntary activities of its members. There has been a lot of media attention about the pay and rations of a small number of political activists (in particular MPs) - but the people who attend the branch meetings, deliver the leaflets and knock up voters to get them to vote are volunteers. I am not arguing that civic life should be organised purely along political lines- but that politics is part of civil society, and so needs to be part of the tapestry.

The third issue we have to address is the partiality of civil society. Being associative does require being partial. If you are a Catholic you believe that you have the true faith in contrast with others - say a Protestant or a Muslim. But equally if you were a Muslim you would have the same view re Catholics or Protestants. People can talk about the common elements between faiths, or shared views by faith communities as opposed to those with no faith. People can also talk about shared values irrespective or a belief in any faith. But the fact remains that people of a shared faith believe they know something more important than people of others faiths. At the other end of the spectrum, there are few football fans with a no interest in a particular club. You want your club to win (and at minimum by implication, but often more explicitly, your opponents to lose). You see this most tribally at any derby game.

The question that partiality throws up is one about identity: with whom do I identify and about what?

Identity

Identity politics has become one of the more contentious issues of recent times. Its proponents have argued that identity has become perhaps the defining issue of the age. Over time we have seen more and more specific definitions of what that identity might be. Here I want to briefly summarise some of those notions of identity, and then use that to indicate some key issues to help us frame questions about civil society.

Let's start with the question of national identity. There is some consensus that the 19th century saw an explosion of interest and focus on national identity. There is less agreement about the reasons why it happened. The nationalist cause normally manifested itself in arguments around the past and a desire to renew a national identity which had been "trodden" or "shaped" or either by occupation (for instance Ireland)or the "dismemberment" of the nation (Italy and Germany would be examples- though neither had historically been one country). The difficulty with references to the past was of course that movements of people meant there were few places where populations remained static- so places that were symbolic in one tradition become the homes of people in a different tradition. As an example consider the Battle of Kosovo in 1389. The result of the battle could be described as at best a draw, but in reality a defeat for the Serbians. However the battle took on a greater symbolic significance in the 19th century explosion of Serbian nationalism. However today Kosovo is primarily the home of Albanian Muslims.

Perhaps one of the most influential books on nationalism is Benedict Anderson's *Imagined Communities.*[29] Its title gives you a pretty good summary of his view. For him, 'in Western Europe the eighteenth century marks not only the dawn of the age of nationalism, but also the dusk of religious modes of thought... What then was required was a secular transformation of fatality into continuity, contingency into meaning.'[30] For Anderson a nation is 'an imagined political community (that is) imagined as both inherently limited and sovereign.'[31] Though this analysis is most associated with left-of-centre thinkers - Eric Hobsbawn for instance[32] - this approach is also found elsewhere. Hugh Trevor-Roper wrote of the invention of Scotland, and many of argued that Sir Walter Scott's books were critical to the

---

[29] See Benedict Anderson, *Imagined Communities: Reflections on the Origin and Spread of Nationalism* (London: Verso, rev. 1991 ed.).
[30] *Ibid.,* p. 51.
[31] *Ibid.,* p. 63.
[32] See Eric Hobsbawm, *The Age of Capital: Europe, 1848-1875* (London: Weidenfeld & Nicholson, 1962).

development of a Scottish identity.[33] The trenchant analysis of these critics is important in challenging assumptions of long-standing, self-recognising races. The 1776 American Declaration of Independence, for instance, talks of 'the people.' Only in the 1789 Constitution is there a reference to the nation, again indicating this evolution of thought during the eighteenth century. With the decline of empires within Europe – if not of European empires elsewhere – nation and race also became entangled. (As an aside, with the demise of the USSR, the United Kingdom remains the one country not described in terms asserting some claim national or to racial identity). Anderson, however, is keen to distinguish nationalism from racism: 'Nationalism thinks in terms of historical destinies, while racism dreams of eternal contaminations.'[34]

There remains one race whose story gives a rather different twist on this analysis, and that is the story of the Jewish race. Firstly, national consciousness is rooted in a longer history ('God's chosen race'), but secondly, the story of the Jews reminds us that race is not just self-defining, but also 'other'-defining. Throughout history, some elements of Jewish society attempted assimilation, and indeed often change of religion. But the instigators of deportations, pogroms or concentration camps cared little for these niceties in dealing out their proposed solutions.[35] National identity is thus a social phenomenon, defined in part by some attempt to distinguish one group of people from another by those people, and in part by others identifying a 'them.'

The next significant 'identity' development, more associated with the nineteenth century, was that of class consciousness. For Marxist historians, this had inevitability rooted in economic status, but for contemporaries this was much less clear. Indeed, for much of the last century, the UK's trade union organisation was about distinguishing one group of workers from another, and unions would effectively segregate around gradings in business. Indeed, to this day, the railway trade unions remain so demarcated. Historically, the National Union of Mine Workers was strongly linked to progressive nationalists within the Liberal Party, and as late as 1910, its candidates stood as Liberals (or 'Lib-Labbers'). That sixteen years later the NUM should have migrated to the most radical of unions says as much about the

---

[33] See the posthumously-published Hugh Trevor-Roper, *The Invention of Scotland: Myth and History* (New Haven, Connecticut: Yale University Press, 2008).

[34] Benedict Anderson, *Imagined Communities: Reflections on the Origin and Spread of Nationalism* (London: Verso, rev. 1991 ed.), p. 149.

[35] There is an extensive literature on the experiences of Jewish settlers, refugees and migrants expelled by various 'pogroms' over the centuries; for instance, for the British experience, see David Feldman, *Englishmen and Jews: Social Relations and Political Culture, 1840-1914* (New Haven, Connecticut: Yale University Press, 1994).

changing conditions of the industry, as to any increase in militant self-consciousness. In Belgium, we see the evolution of such institutions not around a class structure per se, but more around the linguistic/religious dividing line. Meanwhile, in Ireland, attempts to create strong class cultures failed to secure momentum, with working class northern Protestants instead focusing on a unionist agenda, whilst in the republic, Fianna Fail became the home for most working-class Catholics, particularly in Dublin.

In the countdown to and through the first few days of the First World War, there were calls for international working class solidarity; but instead, there was mass popular support for action, and in Britain there was large voluntary recruitment into the army. So again, we see not any inevitability about identity, but rather evidence that identity is shaped in social situations, with some view about whom the 'other' is.

'Identity politics' has certainly moved more centre stage. Many activists have tried to frame political debate through the perspective of some aspect of identity; so we have people talk of disability politics, or sexual orientation. Sometimes, this agenda is driven by activists within particular groups, trying to put the agenda on the map. But also we see people trying to do so for other reasons, i.e. about 'the other'.

One of the more problematic issues in Britain has been the question of cultural agenda: particularly in relation to Islamophobia. Historically, there has always been some strand of racism in British society, even when (and arguably particularly when) Britain was a less racially diverse nation. This was not just about colour – as recently as the 1960s you could see signs in windows of houses with rooms to let saying saying 'No Blacks, No Dogs, No Irish' – but within the British Empire, the colour demarcation was clear. There was an old, white Commonwealth, India, and then the colonies with a majority black population, where in many of those colonies Indian communities were exported to run some basic businesses or parts of the infrastructure. Post-decolonisation, the 1970s saw the emergence of the National Front, with a viciously racist agenda. With the demise of the NF and the subsequent emergence of the BNP, however, the language moved more into so-called 'cultural values' sphere, and in particular, towards a strong focus on Islamophobia.

Joseph Nye is one of the most influential foreign policy experts in the world today. He argues that 'Leaders are identity entrepreneurs who increase their power by activating and mobilising some of their followers' multiple identities at the cost of others.'[36]

---

[35] Joseph S. Nye Jr., *The Powers to Lead* (Oxford: Oxford University Press, 2008), pp. 46-7.

Howard Gardner is the psychologist famous for putting the idea of multiple intelligence on the map. His his take on the identity challenge is as follows:

> The heroes of my study turn out to be Mahatma Gandhi and Jean Monnet, two men who attempted to enlarge the sense of "we". Monnet devoted his life to the proposition that Europe need not remain a set of battling nations...Gandhi devoted his life to exemplifying the idea that individuals of different races and ethnicities need not oppose one another violently.[37]

What I want to argue against is a simple 'clash of civilisations' thesis, of the type most associated with Samuel Huntington.[38] Instead let's consider Amartya Sen:

> In our normal lives we see ourselves as members of a variety of groups- we belong to them all. The same person can be, without any contradiction, an American citizen, of Caribbean origin, with African ancestry, a Christian, a liberal, a woman, a vegetarian, a long-distance runner, a historian, a schoolteacher, a novelist, a feminist, a heterosexual, a believer in gay and lesbian rights, a theatre lover, an environmental activist, a tennis fan, a jazz musician, and someone who is deeply committed to the view that there are intelligent beings in outer space with whom it is extremely urgent to talk (preferably in English).[39]

Politics, civil society and morality

Politicians as a breed do not get high approval ratings from citizens. No doubt the 2009 MPs' expenses saga has contributed to recent views of politicians, but this phenomenon has a much longer history. Look at the political cartoons of the eighteenth and nineteenth centuries, going back to Gillray and Hogarth and Rowlandson – the consistent theme is, at best, a very low esteem for politicians, and at worst a presumption that they are corrupt. Without doubt there are some corrupt politicians, just as there are corrupt businessmen, shop assistants, builders etc. Viewed from an international stage, the striking thing about British politics is how small the corruption is, and how few politicians act in such a way. However, from time to time we get a call for a new breed of politicians, politicians who put principle and ethics first.

---

[37] Howard Gardner, 'Leadership: A Cognitive Perspective', *SAIS Review*, 16:2 (Summer-Fall 1996), pp.109-22.
[38] Samuel P. Huntington, 'The Clash of Civilizations?', *Foreign Affairs*, 72:3 (Summer 1993) pp. 22-49.
[39] Amartya Sen, *Identity and Violence: The Illusion of Destiny* (New York: W.W. Norton, 2006), pp. 4-5.

In America, this line of argument is often described as the promotion of deliberative democracy. Against it is a strong tradition of political 'realism'. Whilst we clearly do not want lots of politicians who are amoral, I want to argue that instead of seeing these as total opposites, we should instead look at the spectrum of approaches which politicians have to adopt in different circumstances.

Perhaps the most hard-line 'realist' was Lenin. His famous maxim was "Who Whom". For Lenin what mattered was who benefits, and who pays. Raymond Geuss, Emeritus Professor of Philosophy at Cambridge, is a leading modern exponent of political realism. He argues that political 'philosophy must be realist. It should 'be concerned in the first instance not with how people ought ideally to act', which is very much the "deliberative democracy" thesis. 'but rather with the way the social, political, etc institutions actually operate at some given time, and what really does move human beings to act in given circumstances.'[40]

Using Lenin as the advocate of this position might seem to imply that realists are all hard-nosed thugs, but there is a much wider realist argument. This is about accepting that a lot of relationships with voters are transactional: 'vote for me/my party and you will get x in return'. There is a long-established political maxim that oppositions do not win elections, governments lose them. I can think of no example of a government losing power because the domestic economy was growing too fast. More generally, within class-based politics, the expectation was that the winners would defend their supporters. Late in his life, Gladstone described the Conservative Party he had belonged to in his youth as standing on two legs: the good leg a reverence for history and tradition, and the lame leg a reverence for class interest. (He then twisted the knife by saying that by the 1880s, only class interest remained.)

British politicians often take a close interest in American politics – but American politics actually has more parallels with Irish politics. It was Irish emigrants who brought to America what came to be known as 'pork barrel' politics. And 'pork barrel' politics remains critical to understanding what still happens today in Congress. You can be a fervent 'Tea Party' activist, determined to slash public expenditure; but to get re-elected you still try and ensure that as much of that expenditure as possible gets spent in your district or state. Irish elections run on an STV system within multi-member constituencies. But if you watch any election, you find that for the two main parties in particular, the candidates do not fight

---

[40] Raymond Geuss, *Philosophy and Real Politics* (Princeton, New Jersey: Princeton University Press, 2008), p. 9.

across the whole constituency, but for closely designated parts of that constituency. You become the candidate for one town, your colleague's candidates for others. Each candidate aims to develop a relationship with voters based on delivering for that place. Collectively, they aim to win as many of the seats as possible in that constituency, achieved by ensuring as few 'wasted' votes as possible. This tradition has passed to Northern Ireland, whose assembly elections follow this path; and where Sinn Fein even achieved the "impossible" result under STV of electing all five candidates in Belfast West.

Similarly, in this 'realist' space we find Thomas Hobbes. For Hobbes, the world is pretty brutal, so you use power to enforce order and discipline.[41] For Hobbes, your job in power was not to become nice and concerned, but to be ruthless and focused. Advocates of this position are realists, but they would also say that they create the conditions which allow people to flourish. Perhaps the most memorable summary of that argument is the Harry Lime 'cuckoo clock speech' in *The Third Man* – a speech improvised on set by Orson Welles, who played the character of Lime:

> In Italy, for thirty years under the Borgias, they had warfare, terror, murder and bloodshed, but they produced Michelangelo, Leonardo da Vinci and the Renaissance. In Switzerland, they had brotherly love, they had 500 years of democracy and peace – and what did that produce? The cuckoo clock![42]

Welles subsequently told his biographer 'When the picture came out, the Swiss very nicely pointed out to me, that they've never made any cuckoo clocks.'[43]

Moving slightly along the spectrum, we encounter Machiavelli. Today, to be described as Machiavellian is not normally a term of praise. But if we go back to what he wrote about in The Prince, his core argument was that good intentions are not enough; if you want to achieve outcomes, you have to understand the wider world in which you operate, and how your actions are interpreted by others.[44] This is not far removed from the Jesuit argument about the ends justifying the means. This is an argument which says by all means have noble objectives, but you may have to get your hands dirty to achieve them.

As an illustration, consider the Second World War. Most Britons now believe that their country was right to fight Nazi Germany. When Germany invaded Russia,

---

[41] See Thomas Hobbes, *Leviathan, Parts I and II* (Plymouth: Broadway Press, 2005 [first pub. 1651]).

[42] Graham Greene, *The Third Man: Original Screenplay* (London: Faber and Faber, 1973), p. 100n.

[43] Orson Welles and Peter Bogdanovich, *This is Orson Welles* (New York: Da Capo Press, 1998 [rev. 2nd ed.]), p. 189.

[44] See Niccolo Macchiavelli, *The Prince* (London: Longman, 2003 [first pub. 1532]).

there was popular support for helping Russia. We now know that in the scheme of things, Hitler was a more efficient mass-murderer than Stalin, but Stalin certainly ran him close, so a more modern argument for that support is the old maxim that 'my enemy's enemy is my friend.' However, this certainly tests an argument about a purely 'ethical' foreign policy. Now let us come to the end of the war, and the decision to drop the atomic bombs: it is pretty clear that Truman certain in his mind what he was doing, and had no subsequent regrets. He simply was not prepared to see the scale of American lives lost to win a 'conventional' campaign when the loss of a significant (but much smaller) number of civilians could achieve the same result a lot quicker.

Michael Walzer is one of our leading 'communitarian' thinkers, but also one who understands political realism. In his influential *Just and Unjust Wars*, he argues that political rulers are obliged to put the safety of their community ahead of other 'absolute' moral obligations (e.g. not to torture or kill the innocent), and that 'no government can put the life of the community and all its members at risk, so long as there are actions available to it, even immoral actions, that would avoid or reduce the risk...This is what political leaders are for; that is their first task.'[45]

These dilemmas remain today. For instance, ongoing involvement in Afghanistan requires engagement with Pakistan, with all the compromises that entails.

Let us now consider when, if ever, it is justifiable for a politician to lie. Cardinal Richelieu had a maxim: 'To know how to dissemble is the knowledge of kings.'[46] Plato argued in *The Republic* that there were times when rulers should lie to their citizens where it was for the citizen's benefit.[47] Immanuel Kant, on the other hand, condemned lying under any circumstances.[48] During the Matrix Churchill trial, Alan Clark MP famously used the phrase in the witness stand that he had been 'economical with the actualité.'[49] In that particular instance, I do think Clark had crossed the line, but consider, in the days of fixed currencies, statements by Chancellors prior to any devaluation. It is always thought impossible – until it happens. The forms of words used may vary, but what Chancellors always knew was that if they admitted it was about to happen before it happened, there would have

---

[45] Michael Walzer, *Just and Unjust Wars: A Moral Argument With Historical Illustrations* (New York: Basic Books, 1972 [rev. 2006 ed.]), pp. XX.

[46] Cardinal De Richelieu [trans. Jean Desmarets de Saint-Sorlin], *Mirame* (London: Nabu Press, 2012 [first pub. c.1625])

[47] Plato [trans. Benjamin Jowett], *The Republic* (London: Anchor Books, 1980 [first pub. in Ancient Greek, c.380 BC]), pp. 27-8.

[48] See the argument of Immanuel Kant [Mary Gregor and Jens Timmermann eds.], *Groundwork of the Metaphysics of Morals* (Cambridge: Cambridge University Press, 2012 [first pub. 1785])

[49] 'Alan Clark: Obituary', *Daily Telegraph*, September 8, 1999, p. 26.

been an immediate serious run on the currency, which would make the situation even worse. John Rawls talked of 'ideal theory' and 'non-ideal theory.'[50] In an ideal world, everyone would play be the rules; but if you are dealing with, say, an enemy country whose leadership has no regard for such rules, you may well be in the game of trying to deceive them. Philosophically this argument sits well within the Consequentialist tradition (which in British philosophy is most famously utilitarianism).

Widening this theme, Bernard Williams discussed this issue in *Public and Private Morality*:

> Hear no evil, see no evil – you get involved in politics for the best of reasons, but you discover that parts of the political system operate under different rules. There is no doubt that Kennedy only won the 1960 American election thanks to creative vote counting in Cook County (Chicago to the rest of us) where the Daley machine delivered votes by various means. Johnson did not leave Texas to doubt re the result. But equally the Nixon vote benefitted from similar (if less high profile) assistance in other key states. The trouble here is that whilst people climb the political ladder they promise to themselves they will change things once they reach the top of the ladder, once they reach there they have either become numb to these issues, or worse need to use them themselves to sustain power.[51]

Another way of looking at this is recognising fights you cannot win. *The West Wing* remains the ultimate TV series for political aficionados. There was one famous episode when President Bartlet was being encouraged by all his aides to sign a stay of execution for a black man sentenced to death for murder. During the episode, we heard all sorts of reasons and arguments for the President to intervene, and as midnight approached Bartlet was with an old friend who was a Catholic priest. The hour passed, the execution took place, and the priest heard Bartlet's confession.[52]

The backdrop to this story is that Democrats know that the turning point of the 1988 Presidential campaign was the Willie Horton affair, where Dukakis was seen to be weak, and the Bush campaign ruthlessly exploited that perceived weakness. Horton was a felon, convicted to life imprisonment, with no chance of parole.

---

[50] See John Rawls, *A Theory of Justice, Second Edition* (Cambridge, Massachusetts: Harvard University Press, 1999).
[51] Bernard Williams, 'Politics and Moral Character', in Stuart Hampshire et al. (eds.), *Public and Private Morality* (Cambridge: Cambridge University Press, 1978), pp. 59-60.
[52] *The West Wing*, Series 1, Episode 14: 'Take This Sabbath'.

Massachusetts however had adopted a policy of furlough (temporary leave of absence over a weekend). Horton did not return from his furlough, and undertook assault, armed robbery and rape. Republican ads were relentless (the issue also that toxic ingredient of American politics – race). Dukakis was caught on the back foot, and never recovered momentum. Contrast this with Bill Clinton's actions in 1992. Mid-campaign, Clinton flew back to Arkansas to personally oversee the execution of Ricky Ray Rector, who had been sentenced to death, despite the fact that Rector was himself brain damaged.

Moving further along, you learn that you can only fight so many battles at any one time, because you need to galvanise support for what you are trying to achieve. To drive through the New Deal, Franklin D. Roosevelt found common cause with a number of Midwest Republicans to overcome opposition from Southern Democrats. But to move ground in the build-up to and start of the Second World War, he had to flip this: there remained stronger emotional ties between the South and Britain going back to the cotton trade and Lancashire, whilst the Mid-West, containing the largest Germanic population in the States, held a predominantly deep hostility to European military engagement.

Next, think of the issue in American politics which became known as 'the Catholic Question.' Despite the large number of American Catholics (up to one third of Americans) there have been only three Catholic presidential nominees (Al Smith, John F. Kennedy, and John Kerry). Smith lost dramatically in 1928, Kennedy had to overcome serious anti-Catholic sentiment to win one of the closest races in American history, and in 2004 Kerry could not even win the Catholic vote.

There had been previous American presidents with Irish roots. Presidents Andrew Jackson's parents were born in Ireland. The fathers of both Presidents James Buchanan and Chester A. Arthur were Irish-born. However these other Irish Presidents had been Protestants.

This issue was seen as a key problem for Kennedy in 1960. A key question was how he would tackle the Catholic question. This materialised in the West Virginia primary. West Virginia had (and still has) one of the least Catholic and most Evangelical communities in America. It was Kennedy's overwhelming victory in that primary which put the issue to rest for the remainder of the contest for the Democratic nomination. But Kennedy knew the issue would dog him throughout the general election if he did not address it directly. Late in the campaign, Kennedy used a meeting of Protestant ministers in Houston, Texas to tackle this issue head on. He announced: 'I am not the Catholic candidate for President. I am the

Democratic Party's candidate for President who happens to be a Catholic.' Kennedy himself believed that he was headed for a much more comfortable margin of victory than proved the case, and blamed the closeness of his victory (less than 113,000 votes) on the religious issue.[53]

There is a wider application of this – render unto Caesar that which is Caesar's. This is about the limitations of the imposition of personal beliefs in a democracy. The key principle about both liberty and democracy is the ability for people to do things with which you disagree. Bertrand Russell put this most trenchantly saying anything weaker merely gives us the liberty, which he facetiously defined as 'the right to obey the police.'[54] In Britain we have (in the main) attempted to separate 'conscience issues' from party politics. So whilst the majority of Conservatives were against hunting bans, Ann Widdecombe – someone who by no stretch of the imagination could be described as a Liberal – was a passionate advocate of the ban. But once we move to a settlement on a difficult issue, the correct political response is usually to see that as closure, even though you might remain personally passionately against the solution. Moreover, even when people of similar persuasion might wish to revive the challenge, it is still often the correct political response to sit on your hands, not least because if some accommodation has been reached, reopening the debate might mean the next solution does not go your way, but in fact is a further tilt against your position.

For the politician to so sit on the fence is not an abdication of moral responsibility. It is recognition that the role of the politician and the advocate are different. The job of politics is to try and find ways of holding people together through these challenges. Here is C.A.J. Coady:

> it needs to be understood that compromise is not only often a practical necessity in politics, but also that it can be dictated by a respect for the conscientiously held views and the dignity of those who disagree with you. This is especially so when issues are morally complex and genuinely contentious.[55]

The American Constitution is famous for its emphasis on the separation of powers. James Madison was central to this, with his emphasis on laws rather than leaders. As Michael Keeley has written 'Madisonian government works not because

---

[53] Scott Farris, Kennedy and Reagan: Why Their Legacies Endure (New York: Lyons Press, 2013), p. 299.

[54] Bertrand Russell, The Good Citizen's Alphabet (London: Gaberbocchus Press, 1953), p.18.

[55] C.A.J. Coady, Messy Morality: The Challenge of Politics (Oxford: Oxford University Press, 2008), p. 58.

participants agree on goals, but because they can agree on specific activities (as in acts of legislation) that address their different goals. So too in "private" organisations, like corporations, the glue that holds them together need not be consensus on ends but can be simply consent to means- agreement on rules, rights, and the responsibilities that serve the separate interests of participants.'[56] This is not to say that politicians cannot be in the vanguard of change. Historically, William Wilberforce was critical to the anti-slavery cause. Moreover, the passion of Jack Ashley and Alf Morris to put disability on the agenda was evident, both in their action and in their whole behaviour. But doing this nearly always has other implications. Quite often, such advocates become known as 'single issue' politicians. Even if this is not the case, the ability of the advocate to take this moral high ground is normally dependent on their being 'loyal' on all other issues. It is because of their loyalty (i.e. their willingness to follow the party line even when it is unpopular) that gives them the credibility. Serial rebels are usually serial failures.

One serial rebel who did not finish up as a serial failure was Winston Churchill. But if we look at the detailed history, his story bears out this argument. Churchill throughout the 1930s was a serial (and erratic) critic. He opposed change in India, opposed Baldwin in the abdication crisis, and most importantly, stood up against appeasement. But he was an isolated figure. As late as 1938 he could count on the support of at most six MPs (there was a larger group around Anthony Eden). Conservative Whips were even contemplating his de-selection for the then-presumed general election in either 1939 or 1940. Robert Rhodes James convincingly argued that if Churchill had died in 1939, at the age of 65, his entire career would have been regarded by historians as a curious failure.[57] To paraphrase Keynes, what happened next was that the facts changed, and so slowly did views about Churchill; although even then, it should be emphasised that Churchill was far from popular at the outset of his first premiership.[58]

We need to recognise the difference between the role of the politician and the movement activist. Here is Joseph Nye on this theme:

---

[56] Michael Keeley, 'The Trouble with Transformational Leadership: Toward a Federalist Ethic for Organizations', *Business Ethics Quarterly*, 5:1 (Jan 1995), p. 74.

[57] See Robert Rhodes James, *Churchill: A Study in Failure, 1900-1939* (London: Weidenfeld & Nicholson, 1970).

[58] See, for instance, the surprisingly hostile and sceptical reception to Churchill's war speeches described in Richard Toye, *The Roar of the Lion: The Untold Story of Churchill's World War II Speeches* (Oxford: Oxford University Press, 2013), or for a more personal perspective, see the decidedly lukewarm diary entries from May-July 1940 of Churchill's private secretary, who would end up being devoted to him in later years, in John Colville, *The Fringes of Power: Downing Street Diaries, 1939-1955* (London: Wiedenfeld & Nicholson, 1986).

At the time of the American civil war, the social reformer William Lloyd Garrison could call for the immediate abolition of slavery, but Lincoln had to move more deliberately to preserve the union and avoid the secession of the Border States that allowed slaveholding. A movement leader can promote a vision that is miles ahead of his followers, but a president with multiple objectives and responsibilities must maintain a continuous dialogue with the public that keeps him from moving too far ahead of his followers.[59]

Lincoln manoeuvred with tremendous skill, first focussing on the issue the Union (and not slavery), secondly using the special powers reserved for Presidents in time of war to 'free' slaves so they could fight for the Union (leaving aside the minor problem that the slaves were in the areas controlled by the Confederacy), and only late in the day did he make the final move to abolish slavery.

My summary argument is that polarising 'political realism' and ethical politics is a false dichotomy. Politicians operate along the spectrum. The more successful you are as a politician, the more of the spectrum you have to operate.

Marc Stears is the author of *Demanding Democracy*, a study of the deliberative democracy tradition in twentieth century America. One of his chapters is entitled 'Making the Nation a Neighbourhood' – a call for return to the (romanticised) tradition of town hall democracy that had been a feature of nineteenth century America. Most of the *Deliberative Democracy* advocates were radicals.[60] The conservative tradition is much more rooted in the realist strain of thought. The radicals also embraced 'participatory democracy', a phrase coined by the philosopher Arnold Kaufman.[61] There was a shared assumption that an ideal democracy was, in the words of Alasdair MacIntyre, a 'network of giving and receiving where all are able to participate in the making of decisions which shape their lives and none are solely the object of arbitrary power.'[62] However, Marc Stears argues that whilst deliberative democracy advocates had a clear theoretical framework, if you study their actions, in practice they operated by recognising realist realities. Stears writes ' "What can I do?" [the journal] *Common Sense* asked at the height of the Depression. "Organize and learn" was the answer.'[63]

---

[59] Joseph S. Nye Jr., *The Powers to Lead* (Oxford: Oxford University Press, 2008), p. 76.
[60] Marc Stears, *Demanding Democracy: American Radicals in Search of a New Politics* (Princeton, New Jersey: Princeton University Press, 2010), esp. pp. 85-115.
[61] See Arnold Kaufman, 'Human Nature and Participatory Democracy' in William E. Connoly (ed.), *The Bias of Pluralism* (New York: Athlone Press, 1969), pp. 178-200.
[62] Alasdair MacIntyre, *Dependent Rational Animals: Why Human Beings Need Virtues* (Chicago, Illinois: Open Court, 1991), p. 98.
[63] Marc Stears, *Demanding Democracy: American Radicals in Search of a New Politics* (Princeton, New Jersey: Princeton University Press, 2010), esp. p. 115.

Let us take another example. Joseph Nye is perhaps most famous for his work around the notion of 'soft' power. He regards soft power as having three key components: culture, values and foreign policies. As with the debate about politics generally, foreign policy debates tend to see a polarisation between political realists, and those advocating liberal (or 'ethical') foreign policies.

Nye does not regard soft power as a normative concept. Like hard power (military or economic strength) it can be used for good or for bad. 'Soft power is not a form of idealism or liberalism. It is simply a form of power, one way of getting what is desired.'[64] Nye fleshes out the phrase used by Hillary Clinton when Secretary of State: smart power. This is about understanding what the right mix in any particular situation is.[65]

Nye again sees a spectrum between hard and soft power:

Fig. 5 – Joseph Nye's spectrum of hard power/soft power

HARD   **SOFT**

Command ⟶ Coerce – Threat – Pay – Sanction – Frame – Persuade – Attract ⟵ Co-Opt

Source: Joseph Nye, *The Future of Power* (New York: Public Affairs, 2011), p. 21.

Against the realists he points out that 'hard power' alone is not sufficient: 'As philosopher David Hume pointed out in the eighteenth century, no human is strong enough to dominate all others acting alone.'[66] Nye recalls a famous post-Vietnam War dialogue. American colonel Harry Summers pointed out 'You know you never defeated us in a kinetic engagement on the battle-field.' His Vietnamese counterpart Colonel Tu accurately replied 'That may be so. But it is also irrelevant because we won the battle of strategic communication, and therefore the war.'[67]

---

[64] Joseph S. Nye Jr., *The Future of Power* (New York: Public Affairs, 2011), p. 81.
[65] *Ibid*, pp. 207–34.
[66] *Ibid*, p. 27.
[67] *Ibid*, pp. 40–1.

Nye has also quoted Albert Speer: 'Of course Goebbels and Hitler know how to penetrate through to the instincts of their audience; but in a deeper sense they derived their whole existence from the audience. Certainly the masses roared to the beat set by Hitler and Goebbels's baton; yet they were not the true conductors. The mob determined the theme.'[68]

Nye further opposes a tight distinction between a 'realist' view that foreign policy should be based on interests, and one on values: 'Values are simply an intangible national interest.'[69]

Politicians are not moral theologians. Their job is to use power smartly, mixing realism and values to make a difference. The danger is, of course, that compromise becomes compromising. As Coady concludes,

> A capacity to compromise and negotiate is essential to political life, but when everything, including character, is up for negotiation then the craft of politics becomes merely crafty and contempt is the proper response to it. This is the sad contempt encapsulated in Huck Finn's weary remark about politics to the slave Jim: "All kings is mostly rapscallions".[70]

A Political Morality?

If we regard politics as a good thing to do, then we might also ask what type of moral or political philosophic framework best acknowledges that. This is not to argue exclusively in favour of one political philosophy or another, but to ask what types of meta-frameworks at least allow those debates to take place.

As is often the case in philosophy, we can see two very different takes on this in the thinking of Plato and Aristotle. For virtually every issue, Plato and Aristotle were the first to address it; Plato usually got it wrong, and Aristotle usually got it right. Plato was the advocate of the philosopher king: we should be ruled by the wise, for they know best.[71] Meanwhile, for Aristotle, politics was the ultimate civic duty.[72] Quite a lot of non-democratic thinking can be traced back to some of the key Platonic propositions, but I would want to focus on a different divide.

---

[68] Joseph S. Nye Jr., *The Powers to Lead* (Oxford: Oxford University Press, 2008), p. 33.

[69] *Ibid*, p. 115.

[70] C.A.J. Coady, *Messy Morality: The Challenge of Politics* (Oxford: Oxford University Press, 2008), p. 119.

[71] Plato [trans. Benjamin Jowett], *The Republic* (London: Anchor Books, 1980 [first pub. in Ancient Greek, c.380 BC]), pp. 83-4.

[72] See Aristotle [trans. Carnes Lord], *The Politics* (Chicago, Illinois: Chicago University Press, 1984 [first pub. in Ancient Greek c.350BC).

Moving forward over two millennia, perhaps the most important political philosophical work of the late twentieth century was *A Theory of Justice* by John Rawls. Rawls wanted to advance the notion of justice as fairness, and strived to square off the principles both of liberty and equality. He advanced the idea of the 'veil of ignorance', postulating that if none of us knew what outcomes we each would get we would tend towards a more equalitarian distribution of rewards.[73]

This was his basic building block to construct the full argument. The proposal was not universally acclaimed (the book, whilst seminal, was also contentious), and indeed Rawls subsequently tried to rework his argument not to be reliant on that principle. Suffice to say that the reworking did little to satisfy his critics, and many still regard the version one proposal as the more robust argument.[74]

Personally I had always thought that the risk-averse nature of his proposition suited the temperament of a Harvard philosophy tutor, whilst in reality we see, for example, from spending on the lottery that many people are willing to risk loss for the outside chance of tremendous gain. However, some understanding of Rawls's life before becoming a don might suggest why he would himself champion a more risk-averse system. As a young child he witnessed the deaths of two of his brothers who, unbeknown to the family or himself, caught a disease from him. Later, as a soldier in the Pacific in the Second World War, he and his best friend went on patrol. They tossed a coin for who would go one way and who the other. His friend chose the wrong way and was killed. Prior to that event, Rawls had been a committed Episcopalian, but afterwards, he lost his faith.

We can debate whether or not Rawls properly grounded his thesis, but what I want to focus on are the consequences of accepting his thesis. If you agree his ground rules, you leave very little scope for politics as we know it.

The unique value of the political process is its ability to provide the forum for these arguments to evolve; and ultimately, to grant legitimacy to decision-making. Civil society is sometimes seen as 'Disneyland', where everyone is happy and living in harmony. This is a wonderful fantasy land, but is entirely abstract, and it lacks roots as well as reality. With a strong political dimension, civil society acquires a 'buy in' for many other dimensions: social, economic and cultural. Only with that level of 'buy in' can civil society tackle some of the over-arching issues like changing behaviour, about which I will say more in the next chapter. Politics operates in the space where we have competing values and interests. It is necessarily messy,

---

[73] John Rawls, *A Theory of Justice, Second Edition* (Cambridge, Massachusetts: Harvard University Press, 1999), p. 118.
[74] For a comparison, see *John Rawls, A Theory of Justice* (Cambridge, Massachusetts: Belknap Press, 1971), p. 103.

because we have differing interests and differing values. We need both interest-based engagement and values-based engagement. These are 'heads and hearts' issues. In civil society, people organise around both, and so the crossover with politics is considerable. A good way of summarising this is to be found in a recent report by Sir Mark Walport, Britain's first Chief Scientific Advisor, in which members of the public are divided into those lead by 'hearts' (ideology-based engagement), and those led by 'minds' (interest-based engagement), with uncommitted members of the public in the middle.[75] The advantage of politics and civil society working in tandem is the opportunity offered to bridge this gap.

Using Genetically Modified (GM) foods as an illustration, James Tait comments on how these head and heart issues play out. In particular he contrasts how, for instance, interest-based differences can often be resolved through providing more information, giving compensation and through negotiation.[76] Meanwhile, in value-based differences,information is often seen as propaganda, compensation as bribery, and negotiation as betrayal. So politics and civil society need to be interwoven, and resolution of difference is usually complex, and rarely linear.

---

[75] Mark Walport (ed.), *Innovation: Managing Risk, Not Avoiding It – Evidence and Case Studies* (London: Government Office for Science, 2014), p. 131.
[76] James Tait, 'Upstream Engagement and the Governance of Science: The Shadow of the GM Crops Experience in Europe', EMBO Reports, 10: Special Issue (2009), pp. 18-22, cited in *Ibid*, p. 131.

CHAPTER FOUR

Demand and Supply

Changing Behaviour

As we came to terms with the long-term effect of the 2008 financial crisis, the first response was a massive belt-tightening by public sector organisations, trying to adjust to working with significantly fewer resources. That efficiency drive was necessary, but clearly not sufficient. Instead, we recognise that we need to do things differently, and to do different things. Amongst that lexicon of approaches, the phrase 'demand management' is increasingly used. I would argue for a different lexicon. Any service user who hears the phrase takes it as meaning 'I am not going to get what others used to get', so it is not a language of persuasion). First, let us consider why we need this different perspective.

Demand and Supply

One way of summarising the post-1997 Labour strategy for public services was that it was all about the supply side: what can we do to improve the quality of what is delivered. Money, targets and inspection were the three main tools used. So whilst the three priorities were famously 'education, education, education', the practice was a focus on schools, schools, schools (an approach subsequently followed by Michael Gove during his term as Conservative Secretary of State for Education in 2010-3).

This assumption that the supply side alone was the sole issue has a curious parallel with nineteenth century economic doctrine: the so called Say's Law of supply creating its own demand. (The rejection of this theory was a core element of the Keynesian assault on classical economic theory.)

Reviewing the post-1997 policies, we can see just how little was done about the demand side of the equation. Now that we are facing severe reductions in funding, but also significant demographic pressure to increase spending, we need to spend at least as much attention on the demand side of the equation.

Looking at the demand side we have a number of options available that would change demand:

1. Price

We can increase (or even introduce) price so as to reduce demand. This can be particularly effective when any alternative would be a significant increase in supply (for instance, pricing for peak-hour tube and rail tickets would be designed to shift traffic to less congested times of the day). There are other times, however, when price rises can be counter-productive. We know that for loss-making bus services, attempts to reduce the loss by increasing price rarely work, because citizens with other choices (access to private transport) switch their method of transport, and in so doing reduce the overall income earned by the bus provider.

Because many public services are disproportionately used by poorer people, there are also other problems caused by excessive use of price. So we know that cost becomes a key issue for some people when considering the use of prescriptions, or of dentistry. Some of that can be beneficial (curbing inappropriate use of doctors time), but other reductions can increase costs later: as the preventative intervention is deferred, requiring a more expensive intervention later.

2. Reclassify the offer

This is the so called "easycouncil" offer. The classification of what is free, or of what is heavily subsidised, is drawn more tightly, and citizens are then given the option of paying at more commercial rates for any additional requirements. Though most attention has been given to the Barnet attempt to develop this approach, dentistry is perhaps a more developed illustration, with the "NHS" element becoming increasingly restricted. Taking a more long-term perspective, we can see changes in the use of public subsidy in other areas on a dramatic scale – for instance, house buyers used to get tax relief, but now public funding is for a much more limited group of people (and the present government seems intent on tightening this further by, for example, increasing rents for better-off council house tenants, otherwise known as the introduction of the so-called 'bedroom tax').

3. Personalisation/IKEA style

Most of the focus on personalisation has been on the supply side of the equation, asking how we can better configure what we offer. But if you look at the private sector, this agenda has been as much about transferring opportunity cost to the customer – so self-assembly becomes critical. You can see this in retail: we used to get served, then we served ourselves, now we scan the products and pay ourselves. Ryanair ask us not only to sort out where and when we fly, they have even transferred the task of printing our tickets to ourselves. Perhaps the most radical transfer in public services has been by HMRC, driving self-assessment and VAT returns online. But overall, we have effectively deemed that the public need help, and so have not had the mindset of transferring as much of the assembly and opportunity costs as possible to the public. Indeed, we even have examples where our priority has been (rightly) to reduce opportunity costs to citizens (GP waiting times and appointments being the best example).

The second personalisation thesis is that it allows earlier and more tailored intervention that would reduce costs further on down the line. Certainly, the results from some of the personalisation of care packages indicates evidence to support this, and the whole 'Payment-By-Results' approach is predicated on this being true. The point to stress here is that we should look at this as much from the demand perspective as from that of supply.

4. Behaviour expectation and changing behaviour

This is usually described as the "nudge" strategy. However, I think that is only part of the approach. Rather, we should cast this wider to include:

a. Designing in change/designing out the problem.

When cash machines were first installed, there was a significant loss of cards. That was because people left them in the machine (their focus was on the cash, not the card, and when people were in a hurry, the card was left behind). This problem was solved by the simple device of your not being able to receive cash until you have retrieved your card.

Similarly, 'designing out crime' was all about recognising what types of physical layout facilitated crime, and what did not do so.

b. Nudge

This is the classic stuff of the Behavioural Insights Team spawned at No 10 (and now collocated with NESTA). It is very much rooted in behavioural psychology, and has been promoted cross-party and on both sides of the Atlantic; for instance, Cass Sunstein, one of the co-authors of the book *Nudge* subsequently became a senior Obama official.[76]

c. Behaviour expectation

The most famous example of this approach is the so called 'broken windows theory' developed by Wilson and Kelling in the 1980s and adopted by Bill Bratton first as Head of New York City Transit Police and then as Police Commissioner for Giuliani.[78] This is about norm setting, and the actions a public body can do to help create or sustain such norms.

For both 'nudge' and 'norm' setting, there has been a lot of academic debate about their value. Suffice to say that the evidence does not sustain either alone as sufficient for change, but I think it does support the case that they are a necessary part of the change.

5. Anticipating demand

Public baths (often with facilities for washing clothes as well as people) became a popular public provision in nineteenth century London – and every one of them ran at a profit. In contrast, every new public swimming pool opened in the last thirty years operates at a massive loss.

So instead of thinking about how to raise new local taxes, perhaps local government should think of itself more as a social entrepreneur and try and anticipate new wants, and position itself as meeting those wants and charging people for so doing (Kingston Communications is an illustration where a local authority anticipated a public demand, and made significant money for the authority by meeting that demand). Under this heading, the mantra should be commercialise, not privatise.

---

[77] See Cass Sunstein and Richard Thaler, *Nudge* (London: Penguin, 2008).
[78] See James Q. Wilson and George L. Kelling, 'Broken Windows: The Police and Neighborhood Safety', *Atlantic Monthly*, 249:3 (Mar 1982) pp. 29-38.

Changing Behaviour

Having summarised a wider demand strategy, I want to focus in particular on behaviour change. I use this phrase deliberately. Some critics say this is the language of an over-reaching nanny state. My response would be that if the public has to pay the price of the actions of others, then the public have a right to express their opinions about such actions. However, raising this issue reminds us of a key point: this is not an apolitical agenda, so hoping that it can be developed without a political dimension is foolhardy.

Attitudes towards this agenda vary. Here in Britain we are more receptive to public health campaigns than, say, America, where public opinion is more firmly against the state engaging in what is seen as private space. IPSOS MORI has developed some fascinating research on generational differences. We "baby boomers" and our parents' generations are overwhelmingly more favourable to the welfare state than Generation Y are. But that needs to be set against another finding, that we "baby boomers" are much more sceptical about the efficacy of those welfare state public officials than are those in Generation Y!

It is not just that we cannot develop this agenda by ignoring politics; we can find a lot of insights about behaviour change from politics. This may seem surprising, but political parties have been at this game for a rather long time. Admittedly, their interest is usually very limited (persuading people to vote, and to vote in a particular way in elections), but they have two hundred years' worth of practice to draw upon.

Prior to the Reform Acts of 1832 and 1867, we had the so-called 'Rotten' or Pocket Boroughs, where politicians used a mix of bribery and coercion to secure election; but subsequently things became a bit more sophisticated, as well as more expensive. The total cost of the 2012 American election campaigns is estimated to be more than $6 billion, and even at the 204 mid-terms, spending totalled an estimated $4 billion. When you are spending that sort of money, you start to take an interest in what works and what does not.

Let us start with some of the findings by Green and Gerber in their book *Get Out the Vote*.[79] Here the focus was on increasing turnout, rather than voting for a particular candidate. They and their fellow researchers were able to bring in Random Controlled Trials (RCTs) into their research (something actual candidates were reluctant to do, until the 2008 Obama campaign subsequently added them to their electoral armoury). The point of the RCT was, of course, to move beyond

---

[79] See Donald P. Green and Alan S. Gerber, *Get Out the Vote: How to Increase Voter Turnout* (Washington D.C.: Brookings Institution Press, rev. 2008 ed.).

relying on the story of victors ('We won because of this or that'), and to bring in objective assessment. I want to highlight one particular experiment for its wider relevance. Here, four different leaflets were sent to different parts of a district (each having similar demographic profiles), and there was also a Control Trial Area (CTA) which received no literature from the trial. Against the CTA, each area saw higher turnout.

1. Area A got a leaflet stressing the civic responsibility to vote. The impact was small but positive (in other words, expensive and comparatively ineffective).

2. Area B got a leaflet saying your vote could make a difference. This was slightly more effective. (British readers will recognise our version of this, the classic Lib Dem 'eve of poll' leaflet, with a bar graph showing the Lib Dems only one or two points behind the incumbent, and assuring voters 'It's a two-horse race, only the Lib Dems can beat Party X here'

3. Area C got a leaflet announcing that most people in this street vote. This was more effective. This is, of course, one of the classic "Nudge" findings (the illustration usually used here is the impact of the hotel sign saying most people sort out which towels need to be washed).

4. However by far the greatest impact came from the fourth leaflet: this gave the details of those people who had or had not voted last time, and promised to circulate a similar leaflet to all residents following the forthcoming election. This could be quite easy to replicate (there is a publicly-available list of people who do vote in elections, but of course, it does not record how they vote). Why this has not caught on was because the researcher undertaking the trial received serial abusive messages, and even serious death threats!

There are other interesting findings. The book is well worth a read, even if it is written for electioneering anoraks and political scientists, rather than for a wider audience. However, I want to just highlight the two key findings: firstly, the need to work through your messaging very carefully if it is to have any impact, and secondly, the group dimension (demonstrated by strategy four above) is critical.

Understanding Citizens Better

If we need to engage citizens better, then we need to understand them better. In particular. we need to see how we can disaggregate citizens as a collective, and think of them in smaller groupings. Furthermore, we need better consumer insight, so that we can understand consumer journeys through public service provision. Starting with the former, I want to explore four ways of looking at citizens.

1. Socio-economic classification

Each weekday morning I receive the YouGov polling data, with its summary and take on the previous day's polling. The data is broken down through a number of categories, but the headline formulation is through the classical ABC1C2DE class breakdown. The political parties usually use the more detailed MOSAIC formulation in their private polling.

It is not just political parties that regard this class-based classification as vital. Look back at most educational literature over the last forty or fifty years, and the primary issue was usually about how to improve the educational attainment levels of working-class children.

Now, I am **not** saying class no longer matters, but rather that **class alone** no longer (if it ever did) works as the sole defining prism. Again, because of the amount of accumulated data (think of those daily polls), we find a lot of evidence from politics. Historically, we viewed political voting through the class prism (though as far back as Disraeli, there were always 'working class angels' who voted Conservative). But in 2010, Labour polled more middle-class votes than it did working-class ones.

Back to YouGov, here is a snapshot of one of their 2014 polls, trying to isolate the influence of class in voting intentions. As you can see there is some, but it is certainly not the deal breaker we once presumed (perhaps then correctly) that it was.

Fig. 6 – % support for Labour and the Conservative Party among voters living in a household where the job of the head is essentially manual ("C2DE") or non-manual ("ABC1")

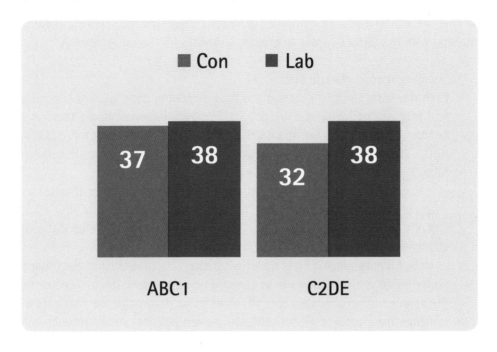

Source: YouGov.

2. Identity

George Akerlof is a Nobel Prize-winning economist (and is married to perhaps the most influential woman in the world, Janet Yellen, the Chair of the US Federal Reserve Bank). In 2010, he and Rachel Kranton published *Identity Economics*.[80] Akerlof and Kranton talk of 'identity economics' as the fifth big transformation in economic theory since the Second World War (the four previous frames being classical economics, game theory, the implications of asymmetric information (the key reworking of Keynesian economics), and behavioural economics. So along with Akerlof's heavyweight status comes a heavyweight claim.

---

[80] George A. Akerlof and Rachel E. Kranton, *Identity Economics: How Our Identities Shape Our Work, Wages and Well-Being* (Princeton, New Jersey: Princeton University Press, 2010).

This focus on identity is not confined to economics, but is an increasing feature of social policy more generally. To understand why let us consider the key elements Akerlof and Kranton identify

1. The *social categories* and each individual's category assignment or *identity*

2. The *norms* and *ideals* for each category

3. The *identity utility*, which is the gain when actions conform to norms and ideals, and the loss insofar they do not.

The key point I want to highlight is the stress on norms (remember our voting researcher). Norms may be what the political scientist Jon Elster calls the "cement of society". So it is the interaction of identity and norms that I want to emphasise.

Now let us return to YouGov polling. Here is the polling for the same day in 2014, but only this time not by an objective socio economic classification, but by our subjective classification of what class we think we are a member.

Fig. 7 – Self-identified social class; % support for Labour and the Conservative Party among voters who consider themselves working class or middle class

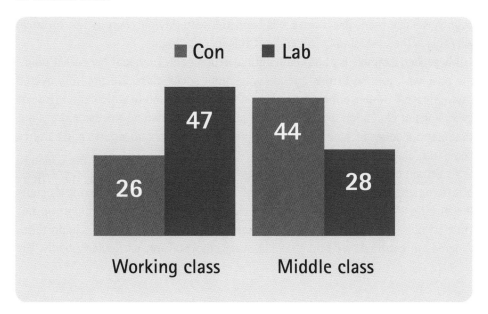

Source: YouGov.

So here the impact of class is apparent. But this is an identity classification, not an objective one. Three things we need to stress about identity classifications

1. There are numerous ways of so classifying people.
These include:
- Gender
- Age
- Sexuality
- Religion
- Generation (as per the IPSOS MORI analysis referred to above)
- Race
- Nationality
- Geography

My aim here is not to produce a definitive guide to possible classifications, but to point out that they are numerous.

To illustrate the impact of just three of them, let us consider first gender and politics. Until 1997, at every election since the introduction of universal female suffrage in 1928, more women than men voted Conservative. (The reverse was true for Labour). Until 1992, a similar pattern was evident in the United States. In both countries since then, the reverse has been the case. My aim here is not to prove why this is the case, simply to highlight this identity impact.

My second example is about educational attainment. To repeat my earlier point, the post-war framing of this agenda was about social class. We then discovered that girls were outperforming boys. That gap has continued to widen and is true at every level of education until you get to professorships, where the evidence is not that men suddenly become better, but rather that selection procedures and cultures come into play.

As Britain became more cosmopolitan, we also started to notice different levels of attainment, depending on which ethnic group you are from. I often ask people the question who is the only group to outperform poor Chinese children in our state schools. The answer is rich Chinese children (so social class still is important). Whereas in contrast, we find that Pakistani boys perform particularly badly. We know this is not about religion, because Bangladeshi boys, or Muslim boys from Indian families perform better.

Thirdly, let us consider religion and politics. The French Catholic theologian Piere Teilhard de Chardin once described cricket as follows: 'cricket is a game invented by the English, an essentially irreligious race, to give them some idea of eternity.' Certainly, religion is not seen as a key dividing issue in English politics. But this was not always the case. John Charmley points out that for the 1841 general election, according to surviving poll books, five out of every six Anglicans voted Conservative.[81] If the Anglican Church was the Conservative party at prayer, then the Liberals (and subsequently Labour) drew from the Methodist tradition and other Dissenters (and Labour also drew heavily on the Catholic Church). This was not just a nineteenth century phenomenon. Until the late 1960s, there was a Protestant Party group on Liverpool City Council.

However, move beyond England, and the impact of religion is much more apparent. Northern Ireland obviously comes to mind, but it is still true in Scotland where each year there are more assaults because of religious difference than there are based on, say, ethnicity or sexuality. The Labour heartland has always been the West Coast, with its high concentration of Catholics, while first the Conservatives and then the SNP drew their support much more from Protestant households.

Stretch beyond the UK and this becomes even more apparent. In the US today .we have the strong interconnection between Southern Baptists and the Republican Party. More historically, as Andrew Manis shows, religious affiliation was a key frame for the 1960s civil rights battles.[82] Manis picks up the idea of civil religion (an idea first put forward by Jean-Jacques Rousseau). Robert Bellah defined civil religion as "that religious dimension, found...in the life of every people, through which it interprets its historical experience in the light of transcendent reality."[83] So here the culture war was between the (white) Southern Baptist Convention and the (black) National Baptist Convention.

Again the purpose here is not to answer the question, but to illustrate its importance.

---

[81] See John Charmley, *A History of Conservative Politics Since 1830: Second Edition* (Basingstoke: Palgrave Macmillan, 2008).
[82] Andrew Manis, *Southern Civil Religions in Conflict: Civil Rights and the Culture Wars* (Macon, Georgia: Manis University Press, 2002).
[83] Cited in *Ibid*, p. 16.

2. Identity is multi-dimensional

Here I want to recall the Amartya Sen comment quoted earlier on, regarding identity. None of us is defined by only one identity. We all carry multiple identities. The only people who get uni-dimensional in their views are those fanatics who insist on viewing others through a uni-dimensional prism (be that Nazis about Jews, or ISIS fanatics about non-believers).

3. Identity is contested space

A good description of politicians is as entrepreneurs in social identity. Here is George Lakoff (of whom more later)

> Language does not merely express identity; it can change identity. Narratives and melodramas are not mere words and images; they can enter our brains and provide models that we do not merely live by, but that define what we are.[84]

This year, being the centenary of the start of the First World War, it is perhaps apt to use some First World War illustrations of contested identity.

At the beginning of the war, leading figures on both sides thought it would be 'all over by Christmas.' Unfortunately, that turned out to not be the case. One front of the war, however, did not even make it to Christmas. At the outbreak of the war, a number of socialist radicals described the war as an Imperial extravagance, and called on workers on both sides to join together and resist the jingoism. Workers joined up eagerly, not in a class war, but as volunteers in the army. Indeed, national identity and national patriotism became key to both the British and German campaigns. Think of Kitchener and 'Your Country Needs You.' But it was not just here that patriotism was key. As Alexander Watson's *Ring of Steel* tells the story from the German perspective, it emphasis the role of patriotism on both sides of the war.[85]

But patriotism could also be contested space. Let us consider the position in Ireland. For a long time, those Irish citizens who volunteered to fight (and often died) were the forgotten people, written out of history post-Independence.[86] The

---

[84] George Lakoff, *The Political Mind: Why You Can't Understand 21st-Century Politics with 18th-Century Brain* (New York: Viking, 2008), p. 231.
[85] See Alexander Watson, *Ring of Steel: Germany and Austria-Hungary at War, 1914-18* (London: Allen Lane, 2014).
[86] A recent antidote to this is found in Richard S. Grayson, *Belfast Boys: How Unionists and Nationalists Fought and Died Together in the First World War* (London: Continuum, 2009).

Easter Uprising becomes the defining feature of this view of Ireland. However, if we pause to consider the facts, what we know is that only a small percentage of Irish people supported the Uprising. What turned the corner was not the Uprising itself, but the overreaction by the British, which alienated public opinion in Ireland. The "lost man" of Irish politics is John Redmond, the leader of constitutional nationalism. In the summer of 1914 he was the victor, having gained passage of the Government of Ireland Act 1914, granting home rule in Ireland. By 1918 he was an irrelevance.

My third example comes from Sean McMeekin's account in *The Berlin-Baghdad Express*. The Germans may have been proud nationalists at home, but in the Middle East they were keener on promoting Jihad, and trying to create a pan-Islamist revolt against Christendom (described as the British and their allies, the Russians). This was an attempt to use religion rather than race as the defining frame. Not all Arabs, Turks, Kurds or Persians quite shared this perspective, so this never quite achieved the traction the Germans had hoped for; neither did the railroads get connected in time. One reason, of course, was that this pan-Islamist vision was dependent on overcoming the Shia-Sunni split, which as we now know, is no easy task; but the question of different ethnic identity was crucial. There was, however, one clear loser in this strategy, which was among the one Christian community easily on hand: this was the (Christian) Armenian community who were subject to perhaps the worst ethnic killing in the whole First World War.[87]

This global perspective on identity might seem to make this less an issue locally, so let us zoom in closer to home. 2014 is also the year of the Scottish referendum on independence. One way of summarising the debate is one about conflicting views of the framing identity. For the 'Yes' campaign, this was about a 'proud nation' taking charge of its own destiny. For the 'No' campaign, it was an assertion of dual nationality – both Scottish **and** British.

This framing of 'British' itself has changed. When I was growing up, that was the phrase people would use to describe themselves, particularly if they were English. Yet today, more English people describe their primary identity as English than they do as British. There is one exception to this: ethnic minorities are more likely to describe themselves as British.

The change does not stop there. If you look at attitudes to the EU, if you describe yourself as English (or indeed as Scottish or Welsh), you are more likely to be hostile to the EU than if you describe yourself as British.

---

[87] See Sean McMeekin, *The Berlin-Baghdad Express: The Ottoman Empire and Germany's Bid for World Power, 1898-1918* (Cambridge, Massachusetts: Harvard University Press, 2010).

Let us look at this at an even more local level. When I first arrived in London in the early 1970s, Londoners were people who had been born and bred in London. But today, being a Londoner encompasses people of many nationalities, many not born in London at all. This is not just a UK phenomenon, New York used to be the most diverse city on earth (a title I suspect London now has), but New York still has attitude. Meanwhile, in Holland, we see that diverse ethnic communities can more easily assert a Rotterdam or an Amsterdam identity (Rotterdam's slogan was 'I am a Rotterdammer', not dissimilar to the 'One London' campaign), which was much easier than asserting a Dutch identity, whose associations are about both race and religion.

Meanwhile, consider the recent emergence of combined authorities for our major metropolitan areas. No one disputes that the flagship authority of that kind is Greater Manchester. That is in large part due to the political leadership in Greater Manchester. (Here I should declare an interest, as they say, since my Chairman is the Chair of Manchester's combined authority). But key to that is that they have an agreed way of describing the place – Greater Manchester – while almost everywhere else, the official title of the combined authority would be incomprehensible to an outside onlooker.

4. Value Modes

For the last few years, I have closely collaborated with The Campaign Company, and more recently also with the consultancy iMPOWER. Both are strong advocates of an analysis through people's value modes. This approach was initially developed by CDSM (Cultural Dynamics Strategy and Marketing). For the last forty years the British Social Attitudes Survey has been undertaken. It allows us to get some sense of the attitudes (the value sets) of Britons. Like many psychological framings it is built on the work of Maslow and his famous 'hierarchy of needs'.[88] (Quick summary: if someone is starving, do not expect them to be focusing on writing poetry).

Out of this has evolved a way of looking at people through their value sets. The analysis underpinning this is quite sophisticated, but we can summarise it through grouping people into three core perspectives: Pioneers, Prospectors and Settlers.

---

[88] Abraham Maslow, 'A Theory of Human Motivation', *Psychological Review*, 50:4 (1943), pp. 370-96.

Fig. 8 – Pioneers, Prospectors and Settlers

Pioneers
Think 'Doctor Who'

- 40 years ago, they were 20% of the population – now perhaps double that.

- Focus more on Society than economy.

- Less anxieties re. security or crime, and more focus on fairness, connectivity and complexity.

- Big picture and big questions.

Prospectors
Think 'Del-Boy'

- The engine of the consumer economy.

- Want esteem, to do better in life, to live in a nice area.

- Results orientated.

- New is better.

- Typically a younger demographic.

> ## Settlers
> ## Think 'Alf Garnett'
>
> - Previously more than half the population, now nearer a third.
>
> - More tribal, more "us and them".
>
> - Socially conservative, nostalgic, with smaller networks.
>
> - Typically older, and from poorer socio-economic backgrounds.

The above is a simple summary of the argument, for more detail look at either group's website. Here I want to bring out some simple messages from this perspective.

1. Each value set has different languages, or 'codes', which in turn either motivate or alienate the audience. Talk to a group of settlers about the 'Big Society', and at best they think you are crackers. Yet saying to them, 'People who live on a street have a duty to keep the place clean and look after each other' seems like common sense.

2. Each has a different driving orientation (at its simplest, settlers being security-driven, prospectors outer-directed, and pioneers inner-directed).

3. Distribution of these groups is not random. Thus we find people who work in public services more likely to be Pioneers. Settlers on the other hand tend to be older and poorer, and with smaller social networks.

4. Combining these two points you can see the problem when 'pioneer' public-sector workers bombard 'settlers' with messages written in 'pioneer' code.

5. Add in a significant level of distrust, and you get a further complication (and remember the Ipsos MORI research which says distrust of public officials increases as you get older). Here we get to a more interesting Cass Sunstein book, *On Rumors*. What he demonstrates is that if you get a group of people with low levels of trust, but who also have reinforcing social networks (aka settlers), who are then given messages from people whom they don't trust (aka pioneers), then telling them that 'Something is not true' (such as, for example, 'immigration does have positive benefits, despite what you previously thought'), then far from reassuring those settlers, those messages are more likely to reinforce opposing beliefs, and indeed, to further persuade people that the opposite is the case.[89]

If you want a second illustration of this, consider the MMR debacle. One rogue (and subsequently utterly discredited) piece of research produced a scare. Immunisation rates dropped dramatically. The response of the medical profession was to poo-poo all concerns, and to tell mothers to not listen to the research, and to get their kids to have the jab. The result was an even more dramatic fall in immunisation (particularly amongst middle-class children in London). The consequences of all this became all too apparent with the measles epidemic in Swansea in 2013. As I like to remind political friends, approval rates for doctors is about 91%, and for politicians it is 19% – so if persuasion is difficult for doctors, it is going to be no cakewalk for politicians.

6. To take another example, if you talk to pioneers about patient empowerment, then you will probably find that they are advocates, whilst settlers are more likely to believe 'Doctors know best.'

Grid and Group, and 'Messy Solutions'

It is important at this stage to stress the relevance of the work of Mary Douglas, and in particular, the implications of her approach for public services. To summarise her approach, here is her classic 'grid and group' schematic:

---

[89] Cass R. Sunstein, *On Rumors: How Falsehoods Spread, Why We Believe Them, What Can Be Done* (New York: Farrar, Straus and Giroux).

Fig. 9 – Mary Douglas's 'Grid and Group' Approach

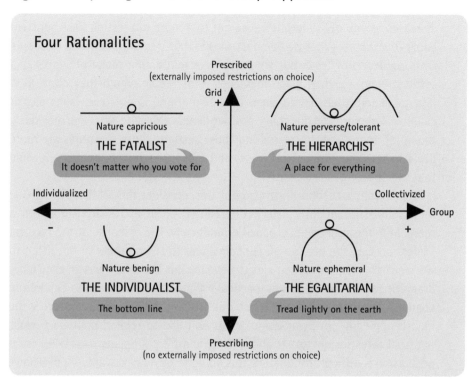

Source: Michiel Schwarz and Michael Thompson, *Divided We Stand: Re-Defining Politics, Technology and Social Choice* (Philadelphia, Pennsylvania: University of Pennsylvania Press, 1990), p. 7.

Douglas was a social anthropologist, and it was later in life that her focus became much more about the implications of her approach for understanding modern societies. In particular, she started collaboration with Michael Thompson, from which emerged what is known as 'clumsy theory.' Matthew Taylor at the RSA has become one of its principal advocates. Though titled clumsy, it is in fact both eloquent and simple to grasp (if rather more difficult to implement). In summary, the pitch is that if people are different, then don't expect the same message to work for all of them. Taking this into policy, do not bet the bank on one approach (which is likely to be, at best, meaningless to three of the four groupings), instead we need a mix of approaches, each trying to engage different audiences. This is an approach which I think a lot of politicians understand intuitively, but this framing gives substance and underpinning to that intuition.

As a social anthropologist, Douglas developed the idea of fatalists as one of her categories, but they did not feature either prominently or consistently in her early work. Yet as we consider modern society, 'public services fatalists' emerge as an important (if often ignored) category. Thompson uses the illustration of climate change to suggest how clumsy solutions might work. For fatalists (who believe 'Whatever will be will be, whatever I do will make no difference'), do not expect them to lead the charge, so a 'nudge' approaches make sense. For individualists, let us develop market mechanisms such as carbon pricing. Meanwhile, those with a stronger belief in authority want strong government action. And the more communitarian or egalitarian might respond best to 'Think globally, act locally' approaches. But the idea that there is just one 'golden bullet' that would work for all is simply not in the land of the living.

All four of these classifications (socio-economic, identity, value modes, grid and group) are what academics called heuristics, and what the rest of us might call 'rules of thumb', to help us understand people. So there does not need to be full compatibility between them. Instead, let us think of them as building up cumulative profiles. Collectively, however, they provide a powerful lens to help us understand the citizens we try to influence.

System One and System Two

So far, I have been considering ways of looking at different groups of people, but now let us consider how we each respond differently, depending on circumstances. Here I am trying to draw on the ground-breaking work of Daniel Kahneman and his late colleague Amos Tversky. Tversky died too young to share the Nobel Prize with his colleague. Both were eminent psychologists, but the Nobel Prize was in economics. More than any others, they put behavioural economics on the map.

The key finding was their way of looking at how we make decisions, and the difference between 'System One' and 'System Two' thinking; a terminology first imposed by Stanovich and West. The original idea of dual process thinking goes back to William James, but their twist was to formulate this as the difference between intuition (system one) and reasoning (system two). In *Thinking, Fast and Slow*, Kahneman brought this analysis to the wider public.[90]

The illustration he uses is about two maths questions. When asked 'What is two plus two?' we can all say 'four' without reflection, but when asked 'What is seventeen times twenty-four?' most of us need to pause, concentrate and calculate.

---

[90] See Daniel Kahneman, *Thinking, Fast and Slow* (New York: Farrar, Straus and Giroux, 2011).

To give another example, think back to when you first learned to drive a car – your attention was total, the tasks were all seemingly complex, and it was exhausting. But once you become a regular driver, you began to do most of the tasks intuitively.

Fig. 10 – Kahneman's System 1, System 2 Thinking, Derived From His Nobel Prize Lecture

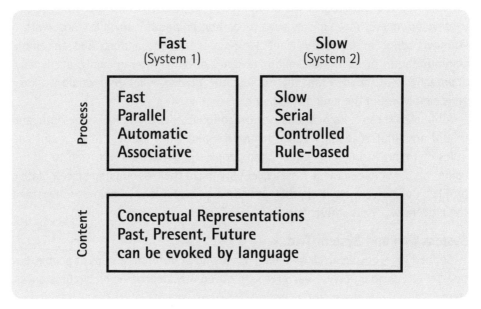

Source: Alex Pentland, *Social Physics: How Good Ideas Spread – the Lessons From a New Science* (London: Scribe, 2014).

Kahneman's analysis then goes on to demonstrate the ways in which biases come into play, as we presume our decisions are coming from 'system two' thought processes, whereas the vast majority of decisions evolve from 'system one' approaches. The book is a fascinating read, and the illustrations are particularly powerful. Some have presumed that the book shows we are irrational human beings. I think that is a slight misreading. To go back to the car-driving illustration, if we all had to drive as we did when we first learned, we would find it too exhausting. 'System one' thinking makes sense much of the time, but the trouble is we do not always realise when we need to switch – though sometimes we do. (Sticking with the driving analogy, remember that when we go abroad, we switch back to 'system one' thinking for our first few days of driving, as we adjust to right-hand-side driving).

My second point is that again, far from politics being a problem, it is ahead of the game here. As many of the most effective politicians learned long ago, having what is technically the best, the most detailed and the most comprehensive manifesto, is no guide to success in the actual election. George Lakoff was one of the most influential linguists and cognitive scientists of his age, but for the last decade or so he has used his knowledge for political purposes. Lakoff brought to the Democrats the insights Frank Luntz has (arguably more intuitively) brought to the Republicans. I think his argument is easiest explained through one title: *Don't Think of an Elephant!*[91] (The point is that of course once you have raised the example, it is difficult to put it out of your mind).

Now Lakoff also reinforces a point Kahneman makes, namely that these two types of thinking are not completely compartmentalised:

> *Reflective* thinking (Kahneman's "System 2") uses the mechanisms of unconscious *reflexive* thought-frames, metaphors, and so on. That is, conscious thought makes use of and is built on the cognitive unconscious; for example, when classic economic theory conceptualises labor (sic) metaphorically as a resource (like coal or iron), or when firms are conceptualised by metaphor as human beings acting "rationally" (using the rational actor model).[92]

Or in Kahneman's words

> The combination of a coherence-seeking System 1 with a lazy System 2 implies that System 2 will endorse many intuitive beliefs, which closely reflect the impressions generated by System 1...The attentive System 2 is who we think we are. System 2 articulates judgements and makes choices, but it often endorses or rationalises ideas and feelings that were generated by System 1.[93]

Kahneman also draws a distinction between what he calls the *experiencing* self and the *remembering* self. He illustrates this with the experience of a hospital patient undertaking a procedure.

---

[91] George Lakoff, *Don't Think of an Elephant: Know Your Values and Frame the Debate* (New York: Chelsea Green, 1990).
[92] George Lakoff, *The Political Mind: Why You Can't Understand 21st-Century Politics with 18th-Century Brain* (New York: Viking, 2008), p. 67.
[93] Daniel Kahneman, *Thinking, Fast and Slow* (New York: Farrar, Straus and Giroux, 2011), p. 87.

The *experiencing* self is the one that answer the question "Does it hurt now?" The remembering self is the one that answers the question "How was it, on the whole?" Memories are all we get to keep from our experience of living, and the only perspective that we can adopt as we think about our lives is therefore that of the remembering self. The remembering self is of course a construct of System 2.[94]

He concludes this particular part of the arguments as follows:

Odd as it may seem, I am my remembering self, and the experiencing self, who does my living, is like a stranger to me.[95]

Putting these five classifications (socio-economic, identity, value modes, grid and group, system one/two) together shows just how complex it is to engage citizens. So if we are to engage citizens in trying to change their behaviour, this is going to be a complex task, requiring quite 'clumsy' solutions to get traction.

Customer Insight

If we want to change behaviour, we also need to see how people actually experience the services we offer them: to understand the customer journey, if you like. The Local Government Association does some excellent work about customer insight, worthy of further study. Here I want to highlight just some key points.

1. For most people, even if people are in regular contact with public services, that contact is only a small part of their daily life – but if we are aiming to change their behaviour, it is rarely about their behaviour when in contact with public services, but their behaviour during the rest of their lives. Even when this might be the case (e.g. a teacher trying to get a child to be less disruptive in class) the solution to that problem is rarely bounded purely by the classroom. (A good teacher may try to explore what's happening in the child's home life, or their life with friends) to understand what is prompting persistent disruptive behaviour.

---

[94] *Ibid*, p. 98.
[95] *Ibid*, p. 249.

2. Different people 'experience' things in different ways. The cost of school uniforms becomes a bigger issue the poorer the parents are; experience of 'stop and search' is very different if you ask for accounts from black boys compared to white girls; patient empowerment seems vital to pioneers, but 'Doctors know best' seems right to settlers, etc.

3. We are our 'remembering self' when we recall how the interaction with public service was.

4. Contact with services is usually at either key milestones in our life, or critical incidents such as ill health, being burgled, etc. In Maslow's hierarchy of needs, much of this contact is therefore for users nearer the base than at the self-actualisation end of things.

CHAPTER FIVE

Changing Behaviour at Scale

In a 1970s Gillette Cup cricket match, the game finished rather late, with the light so poor it was hard for batsmen to see the ball. In limited overs cricket, the usual rule is the lower down the order, the more you go for hit and hope; but instead, there were endless quick singles. Commentating after winning the game, David Lloyd famously said, 'If you cannot score sixes, you have to score singles.'

Looking at behaviour change, a lot of the focus has to be about individuals: the midwife advising the new mother, the doctor encouraging changes in lifestyle, the teacher encouraging the pupil, etc. But given the scale of the financial challenges the public sector faces, the question is 'Can we do this at scale?' Another way of putting this question is 'How can we utilise the latent resources within communities to help in this process?' Building on the previous chapter on civil society, in this chapter I want to focus on what are called "network effects", and in the next chapter I will focus on the potential for social movements.

In understanding network effects, at its simplest level, we all know how usually it is so much easier to do something if someone else is also doing it. Indeed, lots of initiatives are based around peer support and/or peer pressure. Take Weight Watchers as an example. You do not decide to lose weight **after** you join – you have already made that decision when you first joined, but you have also recognised that you might just possibly be weak-willed. The key things Weight Watchers provide are less the technical expertise (although this is a part of their appeal), but more the peer support and peer pressure of your fellow would-be weight-losers.

So what we need to explore is how we might better understand and use networks in our strategy. Paul Ormerod is an economist, and the author of such cheerfully-premised books as *Why Most Things Fail*. As an economist, he is a fan of Hayek, and as such he is usually assumed to be anti-Keynesian; though in fact what Hayek and Keynes both shared in common was a clear understanding that the level of uncertainty is key to understanding the economic cycle. (Where Keynes and Hayek then differed was in their different levels of confidence in government's ability to operate effectively in such circumstances). But in Ormerod's words 'To repeat a key phrase which needs to be hard-wired into the brain of every decision-maker whether in the public or private sector' intent is not the same as outcome.'[96]

I will return to more of that line of thought later, but returning to networks, Ormerod has taken a particular interest in the impact of networks on systems.[97] He highlights some different types of network' and analyses how the shape of the network can affect outcomes. Let us consider several types of these network shapes:

Fig. 11 – Scale-Free Networks

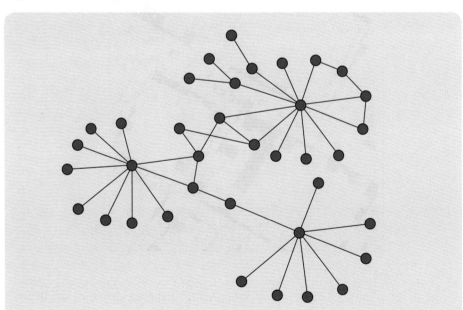

---

[96] See Paul Ormerod, *Why Most Things Fail: Evolution, Extinction and Economics* (London: Faber and Faber, 2005), p. 221.
[97] See Paul Ormerod, *Positive Linking: How Networks Can Revolutionise the World* (London: Faber and Faber, 2012).

Here some nodes emerge as being more connected than others. This type of network is called scale-free because there is no presumption that those more connected nodes have a higher status, they are just more connected. To illustrate how this might be a useful tool, first consider sexually transmitted infections (STIs). We know that some people are more sexually active than others, so when trying to reduce transmission, it make sense to target information at those people who are more sexually active and those places where they congregate. So historically, we might say 'Target young people and bars and nightclubs rather than old people'; although recently, there has in fact been a rise in the level of STIs amongst pensioners! Or for another example, let us look at perhaps the most famous map in the history of public health:

Fig. 12 – John Snow's 1854 Cholera Map of London; An Early Infographic, With the Number of Deaths Per Household Superimposed as a Bar Chart on Each House

This is John Snow's 1854 map of Soho, marking the incidence of death from cholera. By mapping the deaths, and noting the water pumps, he was able to locate the key water pump (the node) around which most deaths (connections or edges) occurred. This is, in effect, an early map of network connections. Today you can still visit the John Snow pub established by the site.

Fig. 13 – 'Small World' Network

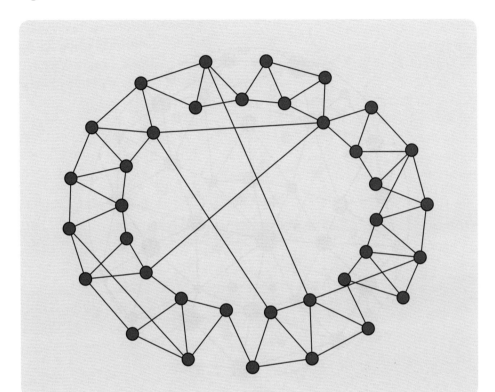

Here is a network where everybody knows somebody; but nobody knows everybody. A village would be a good illustration of this. Or let us take another example: in the 1970s, we thought we had almost eradicated tuberculosis from Britain, but it is now once again on the rise. Yet as of now, the rise is in the main confined to particular communities, particularly South Asian communities. We therefore concentrate our efforts in those areas where those close-knit 'small world' communities are concentrated, rather than on a UK-wide campaign.

Fig. 14 – Random Network

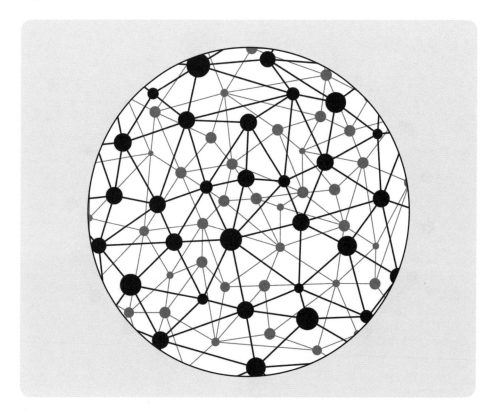

The diagram above is of course just one illustration as random networks are of course completely random in shape. Consider our strategies after some epidemic: look back at the foot-and-mouth disease epidemic in 2001. The government response was to start trying to isolate areas, in the way one would do when tackling a small-world networks; but it became clear that contamination was still leaking out, as it would to with a scale-free network effect. As a consequence, the final phase of the strategy was complete slaughter in some areas, because the risk was that the spread would otherwise proceed to a random pattern. Each year, as we consider how dangerous a 'flu epidemic might be, we plan different levels of intervention (usually vaccination); with the final option being mass-vaccination if the virus is particularly dangerous, and if we have moved from epidemic to pandemic levels.

Fig. 15 – Hierarchy Network

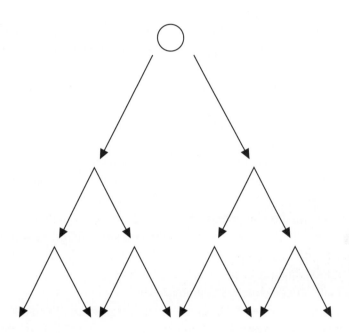

The structure we most see in organisations is hierarchical. Curiously, the classic hierarchical structure, although it is beloved by public-sector organisations, it occurs rather less frequently in nature.

Now these networks are of course stylised, and in real life, they are slightly more complex. But thanks to advances in so-called "big data" and computing, we now have real-time information about the dynamic effects of networks. Another way of describing network dynamics is by considering *connection* (how we connect) and *contagion* (what flows across the ties). Christakis and Fowler have complemented the famous six degrees of separation (Stanley Milgram's experiment which showed that we are all connected to one another by an average of six degrees of separation), with three degrees of influence.[98] They have shown that the network 'ripple effect' is significant to that extent. In other words, I am influenced by someone I have

---

[98] See Nicholas A. Christakis and James A. Fowler, *Connected: The Surprising Power of Our Social Networks, and How They Shape Our Lives* (New York: Little, Brown, 2009).

never met, if that person is linked to someone who knows someone I know. They are particularly interested in public health applications. If my network is full of non-smokers, I am less likely to smoke. They write: 'Whole interconnected groups of smokers, who may not even know one another, quit together at roughly the same time, as if a wave of opposition to smoking were spreading throughout the population.'[99]

They give a particularly dramatic example of this effect of networks by considering measles epidemics. Standard practice suggests we need a ninety-five per cent immunisation rate for immunisation programmes to be effective. However they reference some 2003 research by Cohen, Havlin and Aen-Avraham that shows if you immunise the acquaintances of randomly selected individuals, you get the same effect with roughly thirty per cent immunisation.[100] Referencing politics, they point out that as well as his understanding of community politics, Obama's 2008 voter operation was heavily dependent on effective use of networks. Older swing Jewish voters in Florida (many of whom had moved south to retire), were canvassed by younger Jewish Democrats in New York. Elsewhere, in Ohio cities such as Cleveland, the Obama operation targeted black hairdressers as key nodal points in the networks of African-American communities.

Networks can also generate financial epidemics: witness the 2008 crash. The Warren Buffet annual shareholder letter is one of the highlights of the financial year. Here is a quote from his 2009 instalment: '(Market) participants seeking to dodge troubles face the same problem as someone seeking to avoid venereal disease...It's not just whom you sleep with, but also whom they are sleeping with.' [101]

Alex (Sandy) Pentland is one of the "rock stars" at the Media Labs at MIT; he is a serial inventor and entrepreneur. The title of one of his books gives you a good idea of his thinking: *Social Physics*[102]. Some of his most interesting breakthroughs have come from the use of mobile phone data. These phones are in fact tracking devices, which we keep with us almost constantly. With that data, he has tracked movements across a whole city, and used that data to rework public transport to make it more efficient. Of course, with smartcards, transport officials such as those at Transport for London know where you started and stopped your use of public transport. But with mobile phone data, we can now know precisely which route

---

[99] *Ibid*, p.116.
[100] R. Cohen, S. Havlin, and D. Aen-Avraham, 'Efficient Immunization Strategies for Computer Networks and Populations', *Physical Review Letters*, 91 (2003), cited in *Ibid*, p. 133.
[101] 'Warren Buffet on the Economy', *Wall Street Journal*, February 28, 2009, p. 6.
[102] Alex Pentland, *Social Physics: How Good Ideas Spread – the Lessons From a New Science* (London: Scribe, 2014).

you took to get from A to B, and so we can adapt the transport system to suit your journey rather than the other way round. For Pentland, social physics is a new science, combining mathematical rigour and social understanding. Arguing more broadly, he then talks about high-performing cities as being the ones which have density, proximity and diversity.

Networks can also have adverse effects. Amongst the next generation of likely "rock stars" at MIT is César Hidalgo. His primary research has been into the economics of production. However, he has also looked at who gets what jobs. His slightly depressing conclusion is that the greater the network, the more likely it is that your position in the network (being super-connected) is more important than your ability. This is, of course, the proof of that old adage that it's not what you know, it's who you know – but this time, with some rather clever mathematics to prove it.

Understanding of networks has other advantages. Brian Uzzi from Northwestern University and Jarrett Spiro from Stanford analysed the success and failure of Broadway musicals.[103] The two best guarantees of failure were overly-strong networks (everyone in the team had worked together previously), or overly-weak networks (none of the team had worked with each other before). The 'holy grail' is that mix of diversity with the stability of previously-formed networks. Similar findings have been found in other studies, for instance, in Arthur Downing's work on social networks and the spread of friendly societies in the nineteenth-century Anglosphere.[104] Critically incremental advance is best found amongst tight teams (a French study on winemaking recognised this was why certain areas produced much superior wine than others), whilst the breakthroughs require some element of diversity. As an aside, it is noticeable that in the physical sciences, virtually every significant paper is co-written (often with teams from many countries and multiple disciplines), whilst in *social* sciences, individual authorship remains the norm. That might also explain why the former is innovating at a totally different pace to the latter.

---

[103] Brian Uzzi and Jarrett Spiro, 'Collaboration and Creativity: The Small World Problem', *American Journal of Sociology*, 111:2 (September 2005), pp. 447-504.
[104] Arthur Downing, 'The Friendly Planet: "Oddfellows", Networks and the "British World", c.1840-1914', *Journal of Global History*, 7:3 (November 2012), pp. 389-414.

CHAPTER SIX

Mobilisation and Social Movements

Early in this book I argued about both the importance of civil society, and how within each main party there is a strong strand of thought about how that might be developed. Now I want to widen this discussion into one about how we might mobilise, create coalitions and use social movements. T.D. Weldon reminds us that "Movement" tends to be regarded as one of those 'hurrah' words.[105] I think this is particularly true amongst those on the left; they even get round the 'problem' of right-wing manifestations by describing those as populist rather than social movements. Indeed, if we want to see which movement had the largest per capita membership in British history, the answer is the Primrose League. The Primrose was the favourite flower of Disraeli, and the League was set up in his honour, championed by Lord Randolph Churchill for his own particular brand of 'Tory Democracy' (he had membership card number 1). At its height, it had over two million members, but in truth, it was not particularly political, and was more of a social organisations concerned with organising tea parties and awarding medals to members. When Lady Salisbury – wife of the then Prime Minister – was challenged about this she replied, 'Of course it is vulgar. But that is why we get on so well.'[106]

---

[105] T.D. Weldon, *The Vocabulary of Politics* (London: Penguin, 1953).
[106] Charles Moore, 'A Vast, Loyal Band of Working-Class Conservatives', *Daily Telegraph*, September 6, 2010, p. 16.

So with social movements being as much an option for the right as the left, I will go with Paul Wilkinson and describe social movements as having three key characteristics:[107]

- Conscious commitment to change
- At least some minimal degree of organisation
- Normative commitment and active participation by members of the movement

So the question we need to explore is how can government (local or national) help take some role using social movement to help tackle issues? This is not a new problem. In this centenary year of the start of the First World War, let us remember that one of the most memorable images of that war is that of the Kitchener poster 'Your Country Needs You.' The poster campaign had a tremendous impact, and the scale of volunteering was immense. About half a million men enlisted in the first six weeks of the war alone (conscription was not introduced until 1916). When you analyse who enlisted, you also see significant network effects, as groups of people from a village or workplace joined together. The tragic impact of this collective activity was only too apparent in the subsequent death tolls especially for the first two years of the war. It was not just in Britain that this happened. Alexander Watson's Ring of Steel takes the perspective of the Germans as the war started. They too generated a sense of moral force in their communities: love of the Fatherland. Community voluntary work was known as *Liebestatiskeiten*. Gifts sent to the front were christened *Liebesgaten* ('activities of love').[108] Most of the books published so far have given great focus to why the war started. I look forward to 2018 when I suspect there will be more about why the war ended when it did. By the end, this sense of moral force was certainly less evident amongst both soldiers and civilians. The historian who best captures how this impacted may well produce the defining book on the war.

People might be grateful that at least in the West, the ability of governments to use social movement in this way is less than it was, so let me give a less ambiguous illustration. Arguably the greatest presidential inauguration address of recent times was by John F. Kennedy in 1961. The speech was full of many memorable phrases, but it is most famous for his pitch 'And so my fellow Americans: ask not what your country can do for you, ask what you can do for your country.' (Less well remembered

---

[107] See Paul Wilkinson, *Social Movement* (New York City, New York: Praeger, 1971).
[108] Alexander Watson, *Ring of Steel: Germany and Austria-Hungary at War, 1914–18* (London: Allen Lane, 2014).

is the second half: 'my fellow citizens of the world: ask not what America will do for you, but what together we can do for the freedom of man.') In the fifty years that followed the speech, more than 215,000 Americans joined the Peace Corps. The domestic equivalent, VISTA, was launched in 1964, and was subsequently re-established by Bill Clinton as AmeriCorpsVISTA.

Let's take a British example, NHS Change Day. Helen Bevan is perhaps the key driver of this. As she likes to say, 'It all started with a tweet.' She had been in conversation late in the summer of 2012 with two trainee doctors, out of which evolved the idea of there being an 'NHS Change Day.' Helen is an advocate of the techniques of both Saul Alinsky and Marshall Ganz (of whom more shortly). NHS Change Day won the Harvard Business Review/McKinsey M-Prize for management innovation. Their idea was simple: persuade as many people in the NHS as possible to make a commitment to go that extra step on just one day. They used all the best social movement techniques of Alinsky and Ganz, and for the Change Day itself – which was March 13, 2013 – 189,000 people had made the pledge. In my experience, the second year of any new initiative is usually more difficult than the first, so personally I would have scaled down the 'ask' for 2014. But I am not Helen, and she raised the bar. By March 31, 2014, 702,132 people made the pledge for that year. So it is possible to initiate social change whilst being within, rather than this always happening from outside.

The questions we therefore need to ask are about what tools are required. Let me start with Marshall Ganz and Public Narrative. Ganz started off in the civil rights movement, before then working with Cesar Chavez and Mexican farmworkers in California, and then subsequently moving to Harvard. Ganz's approach can be well summarised in the famous questions of the Jewish religious leader Hillel: 'If I am not for myself, who is for me? And being for my own self, what am I? And if not now, when?' In the 1990s, MTV evolved the 'unplugged' format – famous artists rendering their classic hits purely with acoustic support. My colleagues Chris Lawrence-Pietroni and Mari Davis are passionate advocates of this approach to storytelling. Here we are back in the world of storytelling, following Marshall Ganz, who aimed for an 'unplugged' model with three key components.

- The story of me
- The story of us
- The story of now

As a way to galvanise people to action, in this stripped-down version, the first question is about why this matters to me; the second is how this connects me with the people I am trying to motivate; and the third is why this matters now. As a technique for learning, we have found that at its basic, people can "get" this, and practice this within a day. Like riding a bike, it is important that you can get yourself started reasonably quickly, even if becoming proficient takes a lot more time. As John Nalbandian has reminded us, politicians speak in stories, and officers in reports.[109] But I find that the Ganz approach really resonates as much with senior public sector officials, as much as it does politicians. Indeed, it helps remind people what it was that motivated them to engage in public service in the first place. I do not think that people necessarily forgot that, but they do tend to forget to communicate that to colleagues. On the other hand, if you listen to Helen Bevan, you cannot fail to hear what motivates her.

Public narrative therefore is a tremendous way to help build a sense of movement and momentum. It gets you to Wilkinson's first condition for a social movement, a conscious commitment to change. We then need the organisational capacity to help grow that movement. A lot of people talk about 'the digital revolution' being a game-changer in all this. I would put it another way: social media has enabled us to use network effects at much greater speed, and on much larger networks than before. But Wilkinson's second condition, on the need for some form of organisation, is fundamentally about utilising the power of networks. How network effects can differ, I have already referred to in the previous chapter. A 'whole network' approach is at the heart of systems and complexity thinking, which I will elaborate on in the following chapter.

Wilkinson's third condition involved active participation by members of the movement. For NHS Change Day, Bevan established this with the simple principle that your membership of the movement is conditioned by your commitment to actually do something. In the United States, there is actually a not-for-profit organisation with that very title: "Do Something." It was co-founded by the chess prodigy Michael Sanchez and the actor Andrew Shue. I knew them in their early days, when the organisation was based in some donated office space in the old World Trade Centre (fortunately on a lower floor). Today, it has over 2.7 million young people involved in doing something.

---

[109] John Nalbandian, University of Kansas lecture 2006 with credit to John Arnold, CAO, Topeka, Kansas, 'Politics and Administration in Local Government.'

Mick Cornett is Mayor of Oklahoma City. Himself overweight, and having until then failed to lose weight, he issued a weight challenge to the city to lose weight with him. Over 47,000 people signed up – one third of the city's obese population). (For more details the website is www.thiscityisgoingtoloseweight.com). By 2011, they collectively registered a weight loss of over one million pounds. Moreover, so successful was Cornett in engaging the wider population that he was able to secure support for a 1% increase in the city sales tax to fund improvements to encourage more walking, cycling and physical exercise more generally.

Back to NHS Change Day, here is the graph showing the rate of take off:

Fig. 16 – NHS Change Day, Number of Pledges, January–April 2014

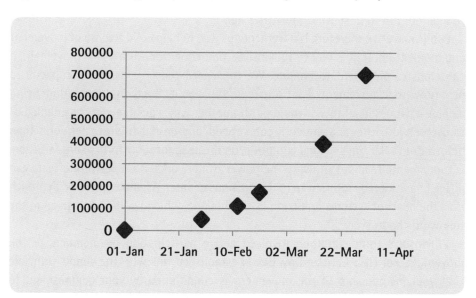

This shows how network effects can interact with social movements. There comes a point when the network effects are such that it is no longer you and *your* friends and *your* colleagues encouraging people to participate, it is their friends who are encouraging them. This is a key aspect of effective social movements: to be sustained, they need the participation of others, not control from the centre. This is, of course, a tough message for people whose experience has all been about believing that they pull the levers, or else aspiring to be the person whom you think pulls all the levers.

CHAPTER SEVEN

Systems Leadership – A Way Forward?

The Leadership Centre was one of the pioneers of 'Leadership of Place.' More recently, the language has evolved more to speak of 'Systems Leadership.' Some of the language this is couched in may seem odd, so let us explore what underpins this, and see if there might be some simpler ways of describing this.

As a broad brush, we might describe a regular pendulum swing between mechanistic and holistic frameworks. Systems (or complexity) thinking focuses on the latter. As a simple summary, you can dismantle a car into every component bit and rebuild it, and you still have a working car; indeed, it may even work better, this having happened if you clean each bit. Yet you cannot do this to a living organism, or indeed a society. Instead, we need to understand the patterns relationships to understand the latter. Indeed this approach is not confined to living things, but is also apparent in many aspects of science. As an illustration, the famous twentieth century physicist Heisenberg entitled his scientific autobiography *Der Teil und das Ganze* ('The Part and the Whole'), to emphasise this conceptual revolution.[110]

Fritjof Capra is one of those physicists following Einstein and Heisenberg whose whole framing of 'the new physics' was through this more systemic perspective. He first came to more popular prominence with his book *The Tao of Physics*.[111] More

---

[110] See Werner Heisenberg, *Der Teil und das Ganze: Gespräche im Umkreis der Atomphysik* (Munich: R. Piper, 1971).
[111] See Fritjof Capra, *The Tao of Physics: An Exploration of the Parallels Between Modern Physics and Eastern Mysticism* (Berkeley, California: Shambhala Publications, 1975).

recently, with Pier Luigi Luisi he has published *The Systems View of Life*, an attempt at a defining textbook for this perspective.[112] Their summary of the characteristics of systems thinking goes as follows:

- Shift of perspective from the parts to the whole
- Inherent multidisciplinary
- From objects to relationship
- From measuring to mapping
- From quantities to qualities
- From structures to processes
- From objective to epistemic science
- From Cartesian certainty to approximate knowledge

To find value in this approach, you do not have to sign up to every advocate of the approach. Rather, it is best to think of this as a frame through which to get different perspectives than those derived from more mechanistic or economic rationalist models.

Although Capra is a physicist, much of the running for this approach has come from life scientists such as biologists, ecologists or geneticists. For these sciences complex adaptive systems framing has become main stream. Two biologists in particular were not only critical to this approach being main stream in biology, but their ideas percolated more widely. They are Humberto Maturana, and the late Francisco Varela. One key notion they developed was 'Autopoiesis', which means 'self-making.' Capra summarises their pitch as follows : 'the main characteristic of life is self-maintenance due to the internal networking of a chemical system that continually reproduces itself within a boundary of its own making.'[113]

The Maturana and Varela work has had a profound impact on the way thinking on systems leadership has developed. Leadership Centre colleagues such as John Atkinson reference this as their key starting point. However, this whole 'systemic view' means there can be no one starting point. Where you start on this journey will influence where you finish, but there are different starting points.

Being a contrarian, I will therefore start elsewhere, and will instead consider economics, as I think this may shed some light on the public policy challenges that are the focus of this book. Whichever way we approach this, be it biology, physics,

---

[112] See Fritjof Capra and Pier Luigi Luisi, *The Systems View of Life: A Unifying Vision* (Cambridge: Cambridge University Press, 2014)
[113] Cited in *Ibid*, p. 129.

ecology or economics, it requires some basic exploration of the specific subject matter so that we can then draw some more general implications, so bear with my summary sketch. Economics might seem an odd starting point, given the comprehensive failure of the cream of the economics profession to predict the 2008 crash, but I hope that my argument suggests why that happened. Additionally, economics is not uncontested territory. A quip commonly attributed to Churchill held that 'If you put two economists in a room, you get two opinions, unless one of them is Lord Keynes, in which case you get three opinions.'[114]

Economic theory has developed both as Microeconomics and Macroeconomics. The latter has been a feature only in the last eighty years – we owe this evolution to Keynes. But the concept of macroeconomics only makes sense if we cannot break everything down to the microeconomic. (The sum being more than a summary of the parts is a key mantra of systems thinking). What happens at a macro level is about the patterns and relations that themselves affect what happens at a micro level.

So here is my take on the development of economic theory. The neo-classical model was built around the idea of markets where individuals made rational decisions, with knowledge. Economists of course realised that neither total rationality, nor complete knowledge happens in the real world. But they believed that the model showed we could assume that markets operated as if this were the case. The neo-classical model intellectually shrugged off both protectionism and Marxism, but found a more challenging opponent in Keynes.

More than once, Keynes joked that he was not a Keynesian. For a long time, most assumed he did just mean that as a joke, but in fact we can see that Keynes was thinking in a much more systemic way than the Keynesians or Neo-Keynesians who adopted his name for their views. Indeed, two of the most famous Keynesian arguments were not even developed by Keynes: The so-called 'multiplier effect' was developed by his favourite student Frank Hahn (although it was discussed in Keynes's book). Meanwhile, the IS-LM model (Investment Saving-Liquidity Preference Money Supply) came from Sir John Hicks, in a famous review of the *General Theory of Employment, Interest and Money*.[115] Hicks also developed a more mechanistic model of the multiplier. Indeed, what is often described as the classical neo-Keynesian argument might best be described as the Hicksian argument.

---

[114] Avinash Dixit, 'My Philosophy of Economics, Life, Everything (Not!)', Michael Szenberg and Lail Ramrattan (eds.), *Eminent Economists II: Their Life and Work Philosophies* (Cambridge: Cambridge University Press, 2014), p. 122.
[115] J.R. Hicks, 'Mr. Keynes and the "Classics"', *Econometrica*, 5:2 (Apr 1937), pp. 147-59.

The core of the Keynes argument was an attack on the myth of perfect information. Instead, he argued that we must recognise that uncertainty is critical. Keynes first mastered probability, so he fully understood the difference between risk (which you can quantify, like there being a one in six chance of throwing a six with a dice), and uncertainty. The Keynes pitch was that uncertainty meant the central presumption of classical economics, that a truly free market, left to itself, would maximise to the best available outcome, was just false. After the publication of the *General Theory*, Keynes suffered a heart attack, and once he recovered, he threw himself into the economic war effort, and then the post-war economic settlement (most famously Bretton Woods), and died shortly thereafter. So after the publication of *General Theory*, Keynes never returned to pure economic theory. Moreover, there was enough political alignment between him and the neo-Keynesians on the immediate policy challenges they were addressing for him not to seek a showdown. Keynes remained focused not on developing theory, but on using theory; remember his famous line about how 'Practical men, who believe themselves to be quite exempt from any intellectual influence, are usually the slaves of some defunct economist.'[116]

The reframing of the Keynes argument away from the neo-Keynesian post-war framing started in earnest with Alex Leijonhufvud. *On Keynesian Economics and the Economics of Keynes* was published in 1968, and the argument involved both the emphasis on uncertainty, and a move to a more 'cybernetic' frame.[117] Leijonhuvfud developed some other arguments about the possible implications of this (which need not detain us here, and on which the core argument is not reliant), but this attempt at a reframing stalled as the stagflation of the 1970s saw the crumbling of the whole Keynesian edifice. By then, the neo-Keynesians had conceded so much ground that the *General Theory* was now relegated to a special case. In this view of the world, Keynes provided the control/alt/delete option to reboot an otherwise normally efficient economic system. The irony of this retreat was that in choosing the title *General Theory*, Keynes was arguing that it was neo-classical theory which was the special case. It was only after the 2008 crash that we saw *The Return of the Master*, best summarised in a book with that title by Keynes's biographer Robert Skidelsky.[118]

---

[116] John Maynard Keynes, *The General Theory of Employment, Interest and Money* (London: Macmillan, 1936), p. 383.

[117] See Axel Leijonhufvud, *On Keynesian Economics and the Economics of Keynes* (Oxford: Oxford University Press, 1968).

[118] Robert Skidelsky, Keynes For a further example of a post-2008 crash reframing of Keynes, see Paul Krugman, *The Return of Depression Economics* (London: Penguin, 2008).

There was however a second key argument in *The General Theory*, which Keynes referred to as a psychological argument. The phrase most associated with that analysis has gone into the general lexicon ('animal spirits'), but the analysis failed to get traction with economists (it does not even get a reference in the Skidelsky assault). I think this happened for two reasons. Firstly, Keynes would never be described as 'politically correct.' Indeed, I think we would now view him as one of those uncles who embarrass us from time to time with phrases from a totally different world. But secondly, economists became enthralled by mathematical economics and econometrics. In that world, and with the mathematical tools available to them then, 'animal spirits' did not quite make the grade. (This theoretical failure is all the more remarkable given the growth of financial reporting where phrases such as 'market sentiment' are core building blocks).

Animal spirits stayed in the economic 'long grass' until behavioural economics became more central stage. So this is the story of Keynes meeting Kahneman (metaphorically). System One and System Two thinking we encountered in Chapter Four. Let's revisit animal spirits and uncertainty through this frame. Now the Keynes argument goes as follows: Given the level of uncertainty we have about how others will act in the market, and given the time and economic cost of finding out information, we all use System One-type approaches to help us make decisions, and for most of the time that works. But some of the time it does not, so we get some herd like behaviour (animal spirits). And then things can go awfully wrong.

George Akerlof, this time collaborating with Robert Shiller, wrote *Animal Spirits* (2009), in which they argue 'The cornerstone of our theory is *confidence* and the feedback mechanism between it and the economy that amplify disturbances.'[119] They also point out that the multiplier so mechanised by Hicks should instead be seen as a *confidence* multiplier. A third key point they make is about the importance of stories: 'Great leaders are first and foremost creators of stories.'[120] In human systems, stories are like viruses in biology. We can thus have epidemics of stories. As the economic story changes, so does the confidence level – and so, therefore, does the economy.

Shiller won the Nobel Prize for Economics this year (2014). A simple summary of why might be this: whilst Kahnemann made a psychological case that economics

---

[119] George A. Akerlof and Robert J. Shiller, *Animal Spirits: How Human Psychology Drives the Economy, and Why It Matters for Global Capitalism* (Princeton: Princeton University Press, 2009), p. 5.
[120] *Ibid*, p. 51.

had to treat seriously, Shiller made an economic argument about how psychology impacted on economics. From two very different starting-points, their arguments have had a surprising degree of convergence. Shiller has also been described as both a 'poet and a plumber'; in other words, he could articulate great theories, but also install the infrastructure to implement them.

Here we get a special twist from one of the early advocates of this take on Keynes: Hyman Minsky. Minsky did not get much traction whilst alive, but since 2008, his thinking took on a new significance. To put it into context, Keynes wrote his *General Theory* during the Great Depression; his focus was how to get out of the economic hole. His argument was that without government stimulus, demand would not automatically rebound from the slump (the neo-classical thesis). The Minsky twist (the 'Minsky moment') was to point out the reverse: namely, that at the very point of the top of the economic cycle comes the moment of collapse, a sort of collective hubris. So if we revisit 2007, we find that the talk then was of 'the end of boom and bust', or the 'great moderation.' We find the same phenomenon when we read Galbraith's *The Great Crash 1929*, which reads like one of those thrillers or children's pantomimes: surely someone can see the danger ahead, or in the case of the pantomime, surely our hero can see the wicket witch/bad fairy behind?[121] Of course in 1928 one investor did foresee this: Joseph Kennedy, father of the more famous (and more honest) trio of famous American politicians. Kennedy Sr. famously quipped that when the shoe shine boy starts telling you what shares to buy, now is the time to get out of shares.

Since 2008, the so called 'sea water' east coast economists at places such as Harvard and Yale duly started pounding their 'fresh water' colleagues at the citadel of monetarism in Chicago. However that was not the only attack. Situated in a slightly more arid climate, the Santa Fe Institute is one of the intellectual centres of complexity theory. Complexity and systems thinking are rather like twin sisters: they look pretty similar to most of us, though they are each very conscious of their specific differences. I have already referred to the rapid growth of mathematical models in economics since the Second World War. To most of us now (and to many non- mathematical economists then), these looked pretty difficult. But in terms of mathematical complexity, they got stuck in a time warp, and when computational power enabled much more dynamic modelling, complexity theory started an even more rigorous assault on received economic doctrine.

---

[121] See John Kenneth Galbraith, *The Great Crash, 1929* (Boston, Massachusetts: Houghton Mifflin, 1954).

After that quick canter through economics, lets us try and draw some wider lessons about complex adaptive systems for public services more generally:

1. **Your history informs your future.**

   To understand the financial challenges we face today, we need to understand what went before. That is true for economics, but is more widely true in non-linear dynamical systems. Ilya Prigogine, the Nobel Prize-winning biologist, writes that 'complex systems carry their history on their back.' In the jargon this is called *path dependency*. Two key findings arise; firstly, that this can lead to 'lock in' (the Keynes pitch about there being no automatic self-correcting mechanism when an economy goes bust), and secondly, that small differences can – over time – lead to very divergent systems.

2. **There can be "tipping points"**

   Malcolm Gladwell's book on this theme certainly reached a tipping point in sales.[122] The 'Minsky moment' in economics is well understood by company finance directors – firms can often make their best-ever figures in the quarter before the recession kicks in. However, I think 'tipping point' may give us the wrong analogy – it originally refers to the point where that additional drop of water tips the scales. Instead think of Thomas Kuhn and paradigm shifts, or of breaking waves.[123] Of course the switch is dramatic, but when we look back, the signs were all there, but few of us saw them. Similarly, with a breaking wave, we see the break on the surface long after it was inevitable.

3. **Interdependent agents influence one another, and their environment**

   This 'Keynes meets Kahneman' insight is true not just for economics, but for human systems more generally. Once you grasp the interdependence, you realise that as a change agent, you yourself are not immune to change. In the 'Adaptive Leadership' work of Ron Heifetz, he talks of leaders needing to move between the balcony and the dance floor.[124] But on the dance floor, we should think more of the analogy of the novelist Anthony Powell in his cycle of novels *A Dance to the Music of Time*[125]. All the participants (including the narrator) are constantly changing their relationships with each other as the dance unfolds.

---

[122] See Malcolm Gladwell, *The Tipping Point: How Little Things Can Make a Big Difference* (New York: Little, Brown, 2000).
[123] See Thomas Kuhn, *The Structure of Scientific Revolutions* (Chicago, Illinois: University of Chicago Press, 1962).
[124] See Ronald A. Heifetz, *Leadership Without Easy Answers* (Cambridge, Massachusetts: Harvard University Press, 1994).
[125] Anthony Powell, *A Dance to the Music of Time*, 12 vols. (London: Fontana, 1957-75, 1975 ed.).

4. Rational action by individuals can be collectively irrational

We all know that if we personally hit dire economic circumstances, we need to tighten our belts, and not fritter away our resources. The Keynes pitch is that whilst this is true individually, there are times when collectively, it makes sense to continue to invest. This counterintuitive insight is an argument for government action at the deepest point of the recession. Political Keynesians often forget the reverse of this argument, which is that this can be made possible by governments seeking to develop large surpluses during the boom.

Widening this argument, we can see that when we are dealing with "wicked" problems, the impact of a series of agencies each operating within its own silo, and each making decisions which by their perspective are "rational" rather than solving the problem, can indeed exacerbate it.

5. Neither the market alone, nor government alone, works

Neo-classicists believe in the market as the correct mechanism, and the neo-Keynesians are confident in government's ability to fine-tune. The neo-classicists believe that the stagflation of the 1970s undermined the neo-Keynesian position (it certainly did so intellectually, with the emergence of the dynamic stochastic general equilibrium [DSGE] model as the predominant fad up until 2008). However, since then, even the ultimate free marketer Alan Greenspan has admitted to some failure in the theory.[126] Greenspan had been the Chairman of the US Federal Reserve Board from 1987 until 2006, serving under four Presidents – Reagan, G.H.W. Bush, Clinton and G.W. Bush. Greenspan certainly has not undergone some Pauline conversion, but he admits at least some deficiency in the present construct.

More generally, political administration has often seemed like a divide between enthusiasts for the market, and those who think government can develop targeted interventions that deliver. (The Blair government believed in both). What a systems approach leads to is both some humility about our ability to "control" systems, and an approach about how to try and "evolve" systems.

---

[126] Edmund L. Andews, 'Greenspan Concedes Error on Regulation', *New York Times*, October 23, 2008, p. 1.

6. Politics has to be part of the solution

Keynes was an advocate of appropriate government intervention. He was never a socialist, but a defender of capitalism. He never joined the Labour Party, and indeed was an active Liberal for his entire adult life. As Peter Clarke writes, 'Keynes was a political animal, to an extent that has rarely been given its due. The big Bloomsbury biographies that have flourished during recent decades have illuminated many passages in his life but have generally played down the politics.'[127] For Keynes, politics was deeply intertwined with economics. More widely we need to see politics as part of the solution, not part of the problem. ('I had a great idea, but "they" stopped me.')

7. Bottom-up as well as top-down

Once you admit that the cycle of 'boom and bust' cannot be eradicated, but needs to be alleviated, you move into co-evolving government and the economy. More widely, we can see that we need a mix of both bottom-up and top-down evolution. Bottom-up policies allow endogenous evolution as institutions evolve. 'Endogenous' is one of those words academics use to give the veneer of superiority – it merely means generated from within the organism or system, in contrast with exogenous which means generated from outside. Ed Balls, of course, once famously wrote a speech for Gordon Brown where he advocated the need to 'neo-classical endogenous growth theory' – something which was subsequently put down by Michael Heseltine as 'It wasn't Brown's, it was Balls'!' Be that as it may, systems perspectives aim to develop approaches that encourage endogenous adaptation, and build resilience against exogenous events or activities.

8. Think systems, not system

The crash of 2008 impacted across the world. Yet not every country was similarly affected. Canada, for instance, did not have the scale of downfall of some other places (which is one of the reasons why Mark Carney was headhunted to be the new Governor of the Bank of England). The dynamics in some of the critical economies was very different. Ireland was running a large budget surplus, and Greece a large, long-running public deficit. But it was the interaction of those different local and national economic systems that led to the crash. Only a few states in America had spiralling house prices (states like

---

127 Peter Clarke, *Keynes: The Rise, Fall, and Return of the 20th Century's Most Important Economist* (London: Bloomsbury, 2009).

Florida and California), but the downturn affected house process across the States. The Irish housing boom affected not just Ireland, but also the United Kingdom. So one of the major causes of the downfall of RBS was its subsidiary Ulster Bank; previously thought of as a bit of a backwater, but heavily leveraged in the Irish housing market. Meanwhile, as an agency charged with sorting out the mess, Ireland's National Asset Management Agency found itself dealing with a major British property portfolio as it found itself to be one of the biggest property owners in the United Kingdom.

Looking back at the crash of 1929, one of the reasons why it had worldwide impact was that it demonstrated the financial weakness of the United Kingdom, and the unwillingness of the United States to move into a global leadership role alone; whilst by contrast, 2008 demonstrated that the US could no longer undertake that role alone.[128] Again, taking this more widely, a systems approach recognises the limitations of any single agency, and that having a clear line of command will not necessarily solve wicked issues, but rather, that multiple systems impact on each other, and so we must recognise interdependency. So we are talking about the capacity to understand the inter-connections, the inter-dependencies and interactions between complex issues, across multiple boundaries – between different sectors, different services, and different levels of government.

9. Promote Norms

One of the persistent findings from economic history is that the greater the boom, the more likely it is that the fraud will also be greater. As it happens, I am not in the camp of wanting every banker to be publicly flogged; but we could probably find a majority who would vote for this. I find the 'blame the bankers' argument for the crash to be rather facile; but 'blame the bankers for defrauding citizens at every possible opportunity' turns out to be so often correct. Each time we (and they) think we have uncovered the last scandal one more appears. Going back a generation we have that famous Gordon Gekko line in Wall Street, 'Greed is Good.' So if government should admit that it cannot fine-tune everything, it can at least think about norms policies, integrated in the institutional structure of society.[129]

---

[128] A brilliant summary of the consequences of this can be found in Peter Temin and David Vines, *The Leaderless Economy: Why the World Economic System Fell Apart and How to Fix It* (Princeton, New Jersey: Princeton University Press, 2013).
[129] A good summary of this argument is contained in David Colander and Roland Kupers, *Complexity and the Art of Public Policy* (Princeton, New Jersey: Princeton University Press, 2014).

Widening this into more general policy, we can see how norms policies go against the grain of much of public administration, where we have institutionalised a dualistic perspective, separating means and ends, facts and values (or policy decisions and implementation).

10. Build Systems Resilience

Once you accept that you cannot totally eradicate 'boom and bust', you have to focus on how you can reduce the severity of the bust, and how you can reduce the worst impacts of the bust. Economically, this would involve creating reserves to help soften the impact, but also taking measures to target help to those most impacted (initiatives such as targeted employment support, or jobs training, etc). Again, if we widen this perspective, we see that recognising that government alone cannot solve every problem does not mean government should vacate the space; rather we need to develop community as well as economic resilience.

So here is our ten-part manifesto for a systems perspective to tackling some of those "wicked" issues we face. This systems perspective complements many of the approaches I have described above, such as the Grint leadership, management, and command model, which is of course predicated on differentiating what is – or is not – a wicked issue. The argument about 'clumsy solutions' is actually one about recognising society itself as a complex adaptive system, with different polarities (such as the 'grid and group' model of classification).

This emphasis on systems (or connections) is not new. As with most things, Aristotle got there first. For once, Plato was also on the right side of the argument, both viewing matter and reality as organic. Moving to the twentieth century, the epigraph used by E.M. Forster for Howards End was 'only connect.'[130] So whilst biologic and computational advances have made this approach much more prevalent, we need to acknowledge that systems thinking is itself autopoietic.

---

[130] E.M. Forster, *Howard's End* (London: Edward Arnold, 1910), p. 342.

That said, there certainly is a lot of momentum behind this approach today. Back in 2009, John Bennington and Jean Hartley (then both at Warwick Business School) published *Whole Systems Go!*, a manifesto for this approach.[131] In 2010-1, we at the Leadership Centre published a raft of documents in association with the *Total Place* work.[132] More recently, we have been working with a range of organisations through the Systems Leadership Steering Group. A summary of our argument is contained in our publication *The Revolution Will be Improvised.*[133] As part of that collaboration, a lot of research was done to collate the evidence base for this approach. Those materials give a pretty thorough summary of the evidence available to date.[134] And this agenda is increasingly being adopted in a number of fields, including in government. In the first Annual Report of Britain's first Chief Scientific Adviser, Professor Sir Mark Walport, published earlier this year, he writes that 'A "systems approach" needs to be taken to the design of regulatory mechanisms to support innovation', and sums it up in the following way:

Innovation is not a linear process that starts in the laboratory and ends up in the clinic, the environment or the marketplace. There is a constant iteration as new things are discovered, products developed and tried out, improved, thrown away, taken back to the laboratory, computer or factory for further iterations, until ultimately a new product may or may not emerge. Similarly, the processes that society uses to decide about the implementation of new technologies and new infrastructures, and to discuss their risks and benefits, are not linear either.[135]

---

[131] John Benington and Jean Hartley, *Whole Systems Go! Leadership Across the Whole Public Service System* (Milton Keynes: Open University Business School, 2009).

[132] See, for instance, John Atkinson, David Bolger, Karen Ellis et al, *Total Place: A Practitioner's Guide to Doing Things Differently* (London: Leadership Centre, 2010).

[133] Richard Vize, *The Revolution Will Be Improvised: Stories and Insights About Transforming Systems* (London: Leadership Centre, 2014).

[134] See, for instance, Melissa Van Dyke, *Systems Leadership; Exceptional Leadership for Exceptional Times* (London: Colebrook Centre, 2014), and related publications.

[135] Mark Walport (ed.), *Innovation: Managing Risk, Not Avoiding It – Annual Report of the Government Chief Scientific Adviser* (London: Government Office for Sicence, 2014), p. 9,

CHAPTER EIGHT

A New Synthesis?

The start of a new synthesis?

The pitch over the last few chapters has been a pretty unrelenting assault on earlier public administration theories, and perhaps most of all 'New Public Management', with its emphasis on markets, managers and measurement. For anyone sad enough to want to recall this, Christopher Hood's 'A Public Management for All Seasons?' summarises that grim perspective.[136] And yet some might wonder whether systems leadership and the like might not itself be an oversell. As I have already pointed out above, prevailing theory has itself been in continual oscillation between systemic and more linear perspectives. In truth neither perspective alone can provide the answer.

Medicine illustrates the point well. Correctly, we have a focus on identifying drugs or operations that will make a difference. We also have bodies such as NICE that ask a further question, namely 'Are we getting value for money for the difference that is being spent?' However, if we ask ourselves why the cost and timescale for the production of new medicines have both gone up, a major reason is not the cost of determining whether or not the medicine has the desired impact; it is the cost of understanding what other impacts the medicine might have (i.e. its

---

[136] Christopher Hood, 'A Public Management for All Seasons?', *Public Administration*, 69:1 (Mar 1991), pp. 3-19.

systemic effect). Perhaps the most notorious failure concerned thalidomide. Originally developed as a sedative, it was tragically prescribed for many women with morning sickness. The terrible consequences of phocomelia in so many children shocked the world. We might think that the drug would now be withdrawn from the market. However, we now know whom should not receive it (pregnant women, or women who might become pregnant in particular), and instead we find that it is a very useful drug in helping ameliorate certain cancers and complications of leprosy. From that more profound case, let us go to a more prosaic, personal example. When I first started going to the dentist, I thought it was about looking after my teeth. These days they focus as much on my gums and the effect they can have, not just on my teeth. It is great that they are taking this much more systemic view; but when I recently chipped a tooth, I was glad they still did a quality technical job, restoring the tooth so that it looked normal. So taking this to a broader perspective, how would we reconcile these two perspectives when considering public policy?

Step forward Jocelyne Bourgon and the New Synthesis Project. In her work she draws on the experience of projects such as Total Place (which the Leadership Centre instigated and championed) but also recognises that some of the old levers are still necessary as well. So she proposes four sub-systems:

- Performance
- Compliance
- Emergence
- Resilience

She argues that we need to find a balance between the authority of the state, and the collective power of society.

Fig. 17 – New Synthesis Framework – Government Authority and Collective Power

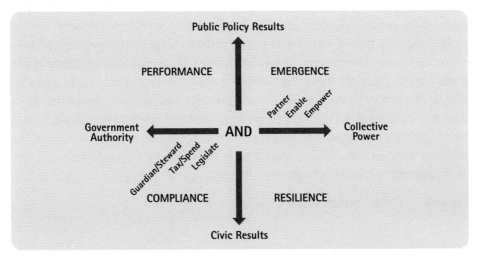

Source: Jocelyne Bourgon, *A New Synthesis of Public Administration: Serving in the 21st Century* (Ottawa: McGill-Queen's University Press, 2011), p. 46.

She then talks of a co-evolving system of governance.

Fig. 18 – New Synthesis Framework – A Co-Evolving System of Governance

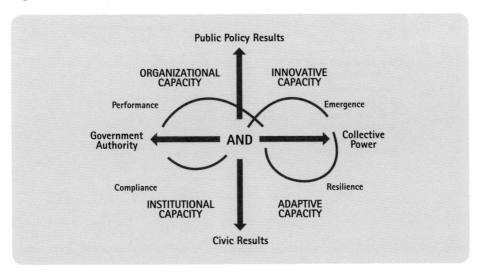

Source: Jocelyne Bourgon, *A New Synthesis of Public Administration: Serving in the 21st Century* (Ottawa: McGill-Queen's University Press, 2011), p. 61.

So instead of rejecting everything of the old, hers is an "and" approach. Recognising the power of the systemic perspective, she acknowledges that public administration has to 'recognise the economic, social, political, technological and environmental systems are dynamically intertwined and continually impact on each other.'

Following on from Bourgon we also have had the Paulite conversion of John Kotter on his road to riches and fame. Kotter is one of the most influential leadership gurus around, complete with his requisite list of what great leaders do. His speciality has been change management. However, earlier this year he published *XLR8: Accelerate.*[137] This is not quite a full confession (he still wants to sell his old books), but he too now recognises the limitations of the old model. Instead he advocates a dual operating system.

He describes acceleration stalled as follows

Fig. 19 – Acceleration Stalled

YOU NEED TO ACCELERATE...

- Innovation
- Productivity improvement
- Integration of acquisitions or global operations
- Any sort of key strategic change
- Cultural change
- Profitable growth

- A limited number of change leaders
- Silo parochialism
- Rules and procedures
- Pressures to make quarterly numbers
- Complacency or insufficient buying

...BUT ARE STALLED BY...

Source: John Kotter, *XLR8 Accelerate* (Cambridge, Massachusetts: Harvard Business Review Press, 2014), p. 10.

---

[137] John Kotter, *XLR8 Accelerate* (Cambridge, Massachusetts: Harvard Business Review Press, 2014).

And as a solution he proposes

Fig. 20 – Dual Operating System

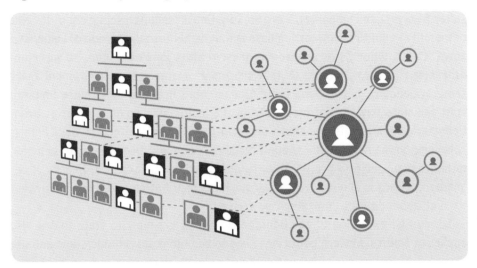

Source: John Kotter, *XLR8 Accelerate* (Cambridge, Massachusetts: Harvard Business Review Press, 2014), p. 12.

I want to advance these approaches further in five ways. First, both Bourgon and Kotter recognise that the classic duality of the split of policy and implementation has flaws. Yet like many other leadership frames, they are rather light on the political dimension. A major theme of this book is that politics has to be part of the solution, not seen as the problem. I recognise that my pitch about the creativity of politics may not be obvious to all; not least what I might call the "Cambridge" or realist school of thinking about politics. (I am thinking of people like David Runciman or Raymond Geuss). Here they start with some slightly more brutal questions, not least the Weberian insight about the state being about the monopoly of violence. In his 1919 essay Politics as a Vocation, Max Weber wrote that a state is any 'human community that successfully claims the monopoly of the legitimate use of physical force within a given territory.'[138] Stark though this claim is, we see its essential truth when we look at unsuccessful states: the clearest examples are always ones where that monopoly does not exist.

---

[138] Max Weber (trans. Rodney Livingstone), 'Politics as a Vocation' (1919), in David Owen and Tracy B. Strong (eds.), *Max Weber: The Vocation Lectures* (New York: Hackett, 2004 ed.), p. 136.

Now we might think that insight only applies to emerging democracies, or whatever – and certainly, it would not apply to places such as Iceland or Switzerland who simply do not have real military power. But physical force can take many forms, such as the power to imprison, or the power to tax. These powers distinguish states from private companies. More broadly, Geuss remains a septic about the role of morality in politics. His starting base is that rather brutal question of Lenin 'Kto, kovo?' ('Who, whom?') As a headline, these realists (or Hobbesians, as we might otherwise call them) remind us that the more emergent strategies might make sense in Denmark, but in Syria some fundamentals needs to be in place first, not least the state having that monopoly on the legitimate use of force. (This Syria/ Denmark comparison is one that Runciman uses to great effect, as does Francis Fukuyama in his new book – though for him, "Denmark" becomes a construction rather than a specific place.)[139] So to summarise the realist case, in Geuss's words 'modern politics is about power, its acquisition, distribution and use...if you want to think about politics think about power first.'[140]

So my first extension of the Bourgon reframing is simply to state that it also applies to politics. Modern politicians need to be both realists (understand and use power), but also to have ambitions with purpose (which requires a more systematic perspective). The challenge that I see facing politics in many western democracies is that politicians, once in office, try to revert solely to the 'levers' approach (which involves physical force in its most broad sense), forgetting how little they work. Instead, we need more of the politics of emergence. Sometimes, levers *can* work – the law banning smoking in buildings was a good example – but most of the big issues turn out to be either 'clumsy' or 'wicked.' Even with smoking, to understand why the ban worked, we need to understand what preceded it: there was a slow but clear momentum for change. To take another (and less successful) example that demonstrates the opposite, one of the major criticisms of much American foreign policy is that it is perceived as primarily about "hard" power (think Iraq or Afghanistan) and not as much about "soft" power.

Additionally, I think we need to think much more about the dynamics of change. Here, let me bring in Brian Arthur. An economist and a key player in the evolution of the Santa Fe Institute, one of his main interests is how technology evolves. Arthur is the leading systems thinker about this issue. He is not just an academic

---

[139] See Francis Fukuyama, *Political Order and Political Decay: From the Industrial Revolution to the Globalization of Democracy* (New York: Farrar Straus Giroux, 2014).
[140] Raymond Geuss, *Philosophy and Real Politics* (Princeton, New Jersey: Princeton University Press, 2008), p. 9.

theorist, but someone whose thinking has influenced key technologies (Eric Schmidt of Google, for instance, acknowledges Arthur's ideas as the basis for their development of Java). Arthur argues that technology itself is *autopoietic* (or self-creating). His journey to this paralleled that of Maturana and Varelo – to whom I referred to in the previous chapter. What makes Arthur's approach so interesting is the range of insights that then emerge from this perspective. His stark summary claim is that 'considered collectively, technology creates *itself.*[141]

You can read Arthur's book to get the full argument, but here I want to focus on the interaction of technological change and society with two illustrations, the first from his book. Starting with cotton, Lancashire was the powerhouse of cotton goods production in the Industrial Revolution. Yet by the 1950s, its mills were pretty old-fashioned. The economist Marvin Frankel wondered why the mill owners did not adopt new technology. The usual account of the decline of British manufacturing is described (depending on your political perspective) in terms of poor management, or of over-demanding trades unions. But rather than giving either (or both) those explanations, what Frankel realised was that the new machinery was so heavy, that none of the existing Victorian-built brick structures in the factories could accommodate them. In other words, the technology did not fit the surrounding infrastructure. So instead it was easier to start from scratch (which is what happened, but not in Lancashire).

A second illustration of this concerns containerisation. Ever since trading began, traders realised that being able to lower the transportation costs was critical to success. If we go back to before the nineteenth century, the transportation costs of goods would often be much greater than the value of the goods themselves. This therefore meant that the goods that were transported tended to have a high value compared to their weight. (There was a reason why the Silk Road got its name). So attempting to bundle goods efficiently is not a new idea. Canals and railways required efficient goods bundling. But it was not until after the Second World War that we really saw revolutionary change. The American trucking entrepreneur Malcolm McLean became the driving force behind the development of the big container ships we see today.

At first, we witnessed this as a dispute between the usually heavily-unionised ports of big cities (such as London or New York), and the new container ports at places such as Tilbury. But then there evolved developments which no-one had

---

[141] W. Brian Arthur, *The Nature of Technology: What It Is, and How It Evolves* (London: Allen Lane, 2009), p. 28.

foreseen. Prior to this, the pattern for production was for suppliers to be as close to the big production plants they supplied. So around the big car plants of the West Midlands were all their specialist suppliers. (Indeed, the Birmingham brand was of a city of a thousand trades). But with the radical reduction in costs that this wave of containerisation brought, we started to see the growth of specialisms. Today, Britain exports more cars than ever, but many of the component parts of those cars now come from specialist facilities all across the world.

Bringing the two stories together, the first is a reminder that there is no technological determinism, the second that changes can be much greater than anyone originally envisaged. So technology is both framed by the circumstances it finds itself, but itself can also trigger radical change. Joseph Schumpeter used to talk of 'gales of creative destruction', but instead, Brian Arthur now talks of "*avalanches* of destruction".

My third point is about the speed of change. With technology in particular, that speed of change has accelerated. Google was launched in the last century, in 1998, Facebook in 2004, YouTube in 2005, Twitter in 2006, WhatsApp in 2009. What we are seeing is an acceleration of change, and unpredictability as to which players survive. Nokia went from hero to zero within a decade. Blackberry might well follow them. Thomas Friedman summed this up brilliantly at a World Economic Forum event.

2005

Facebook didn't exist

Twitter was still a sound

the cloud was still in the sky

4G was a parking space

LinkedIn was a prison

applications were what you sent to college

Skype was a typo

No one can predict where the next evolution might be. What this means for public administration is that uncertainty rather than certainty becomes a norm.

My fourth point is about *The End of Big*. That is the title of the Nicco Melle book that most famously has argued this point.[142] To illustrate it, here is another take on the American military problem: Historically, bigger armies usually beat smaller ones

---

[142] Nicco Mele, *The End of Big: How the Internet Makes David The New Goliath* (New York: St. Martin's Press, 2013).

– that has not always been the case (think of Alexander the Great, or Henry V, or Charles XII, or Frederick the Great), but statistically, the odds were clear. But since the Second World War, and particularly since the end of the Cold War, that correlation does not hold. Asymmetric warfare seems to favour the traditional "underdog."

Now connecting this back to the systemic argument, my take is that whilst we must acknowledge the 'and' argued by Bourgon and Kotter, the interplay of these dimensions means that the balance is tilting towards emergence and resilience as key challenges. Politics, society and the economy are all becoming more generative. As a consequence, we move from finding definitive answers, to creating new combinations. Here is Arthur again:

> This means that the decision "problems" of the high-tech economy are not well defined. As such (perhaps shockingly to the reader), they have no optimal "solution". In this situation the challenge of management is not to rationally solve problems but to make sense of an undefined situation- to "cognize" it, or frame it into a situation that can be dealt with- and to position its offerings accordingly.[143]

Arthur wrote that about technology, but I would argue that applies as equally to politics and public administration. Previously, I have advocated "messy solutions". Here I would take it one step further, in the words of the Pritzker Prize-winning architect Robert Venturi, we are talking about "messy vitality", and the richness of meaning. (His most famous tag line is 'less is a bore'; his whole philosophy an attempt to steer architecture away from minimalism.)[144]

Reading a lot of systems thinkers, one might assume they come from the left-of-centre in their politics. Certainly, if we take an issue such as climate change, then the foremost critics of our present practices come from individuals and disciplines most associated with systems thinking, who are indeed also on the left-of-centre. However, if we take a wider perspective, then this approach transcends political divisions. Indeed, the political philosopher who would be most at home

---

[143] W. Brian Arthur, *The Nature of Technology: What It Is, and How It Evolves* (London: Allen Lane, 2009).
[144] His most influential book remains Robert Venturi, *Complexity and Contradiction in Architecture* (New York: Little, Brown and Co, 1966, rev. 1977 ed.).

with this would be that great twentieth century conservative thinker, Michael Oakeshott. His argument was simply that the job of politics was to keep the ship of state afloat. He was deeply sceptical of "rational" policy interventions aiming to achieve specific outcomes, and instead he insisted that we recognised that none of us could really presume we could be in control.

This brings me to a third change from the normal systems narrative. By this point, in many of the key texts there comes the pitch that this perspective transcends traditional politics. By contrast I would argue that this perspective actually *enhances* the role of politics at its best.

One of the issues of the 'and' approach – or we could call it the dual-control approach – is that it raises the question of the role of leaders. Public sector leaders evolve through classic bureaucratic structures. That culture remains pervasive (in the civil service, for example, people are often referred to not by their role, but by their rank). But now we need people to operate both in that world, and in the world of networks. Here I want to point out that bridging that divide has been much more in the experience of politicians than of civil servants. James Maxton's famous quip about reconciling being a member of more than one political party – 'If you can't ride two horses, you've no right to be in the circus' – holds true for a lot of political experience.

Let us conclude with a return to the cultural theory approach of Mary Douglas and Michael Thompson. What we now face are wicked problems that are difficult to define, a rate of change which gives us less opportunity for reflection, and populations that are more fluid in numbers, and less cohesive in terms of identity, and less deferential in terms of attitude. We are truly in a world of clumsiness, both in terms of the diagnosis, and of the prognosis. This need for more complex strategies means that the balance tips towards emergence rather than prescription. As I have noted, Mary Douglas wavered between a more formulaic four-box description, and a reduction to three boxes (regarding fatalism as not a key group), whilst Thompson contemplates a more evolving landscape, with a fifth dimension

('Autonomy', or the hermit). In *Organising and Disorganising* (2008) he develops a three dimensional landscape:

Fig. 21 – The Morphogenetic Field, and its Projection onto the Control Space

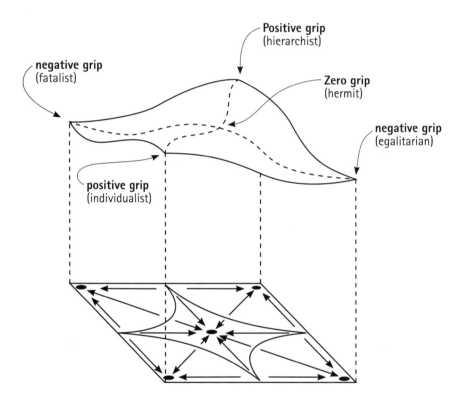

Source: Michael Thompson, *Organising and Disorganising: A Dynamic and Non-Linear Theory of Institutional Emergence and its Implications* (Axminster: Triarchy Press, 2008), p. 144.

Stephen Ney has written *Resolving Messy Policy Problems*. Whilst Thompson went for a further elaboration of the Douglas frame, Ney has reverted to the three-prong analysis. As I have mentioned, I do think fatalists need to be considered, but I think the mixture of nudge and network strategy might suffice to engage them. For the three more proactive groups, Ney has evolved a map of policy systems:

Fig. 22 – Map of Policy Subsystems

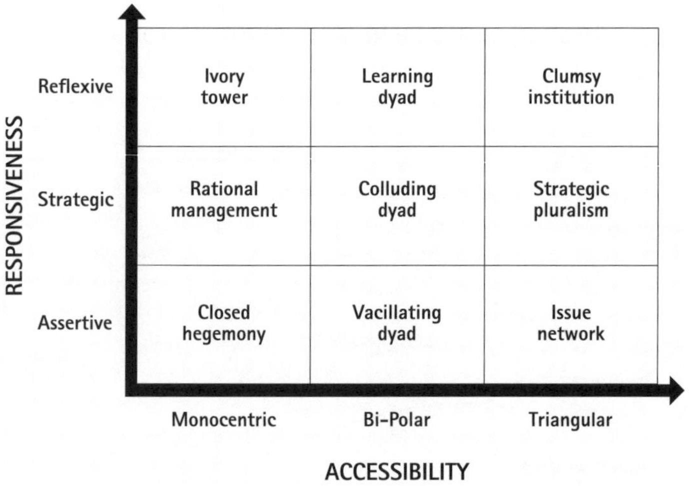

RESPONSIVENESS	Monocentric	Bi-Polar	Triangular
Reflexive	Ivory tower	Learning dyad	Clumsy institution
Strategic	Rational management	Colluding dyad	Strategic pluralism
Assertive	Closed hegemony	Vacillating dyad	Issue network

ACCESSIBILITY

Source: Steven Ney, *Resolving Messy Policy Problems: Handling Conflict in Environmental, Transport, Health and Ageing Policy* (Abingdon, Earthscan, 2009), p. 198.

I think this is an elaboration of the dual operating model. Ney advocates that we 'build untidy (but more resilient) policy processes that yield clumsy (but more robust) solutions to messy problems.'[145] The argument I am making here is that we should think less of a landscape (with some suggestion of semi-permanence), and instead think of one of those evolving shapes or configurations. As politicians or policy administrators, we aim for some intervention, knowing not only that the intervention will itself have unanticipated consequences, but that technology, social attitudes and the economy themselves will also have impacts on that configuration, and on each other. As policy makers, we need to have a repertoire of responses. As children, we all learned the fable of the three little pigs and the big bad wolf. However, the lesson of this story is that building with bricks is not always the right answer. If your challenge is repelling the big bad wolf it might be the right one, but if the challenge is different, it might not. Bricks take time to make, and are heavy to carry. They are very suitable accommodation for a long planned stay in one location. Alas, in the modern world, we often need to be more nimble.

---

[145] Steven Ney, *Resolving Messy Policy Problems: Handling Conflict in Environmental, Transport, Health and Ageing Policy* (Abingdon, Earthscan, 2009), p. 194.

CHAPTER NINE

Synthesis Revisited

To conclude, I want to explore my take on what a new synthesis might mean. Whilst I think the Bourgon proposals are an important step forward, they still lack the dynamic of emergence that is central to systems approaches. Furthermore, neither Bourgon nor Kotter embrace politics as part of the solution. Yet as I have argued, politics and the political process is critical to understanding the specific dynamic of public policy and public administration.

Let me therefore start by drawing a parallel with the Kotter dual control system. As I have already referenced, politics embraces both realism, and normative approaches. Secondly, the Nye 'hard and soft power' analogy parallels this, and I want to adapt that from its usual foreign policy context, to incorporate it into our thinking of domestic policy. In particular, I want to extrapolate 'hard power' and 'realism' as one dimension, and 'soft power' and 'normative' as a second dimension. Thirdly, I want to take civil society seriously, and regard that as a further dimension. Previously, I have referred to my dislike of the binary view of government and markets. However, I am not dismissing markets. Instead, let us look at them as a fourth dimension. With this four-fold frame we thus get a picture like below, and we can see any particular policy or administrative initiative as bounded by these four dimensions. For any particular policy we might see some sort of emerging shape:

Fig. 23 – A Systems-Based Approach to Mapping Out Policies: Four Criteria

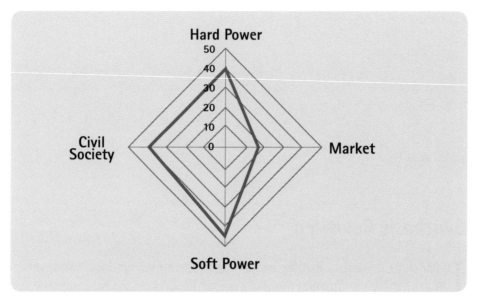

So even at its simplest, public policy is four-dimensional. Alas, life is not so simple. Increasing the number of axes in the spidogram, we now have perhaps eight scales, the additional four being as follows:

1. Policy/Process

The right mix or shape or form of this depends on the issue. Asserting that there is only one way we can do everything is simply mad. There are some municipalists who argue that there is no role for the private sector, to which my reply is 'Exactly how would a direct-labour organisation have invented modern computers?' Equally, those who advocate endless outsourcing have some difficulty in explaining the advantages of mercenaries providing our armed defence.

2. Place

Solutions will often be place-specific. To put it another way, it would be better to assume against scaling-up, unless there is evidence that it would work.

3. People

Citizens are not anonymous lookalikes. If we believe that we must involve citizens, then we must accept the corollary that this may mean different approaches depending on with whom we are engaging.

4. Technology

Technology is evolving at an unprecedented pace. Technology is neither neutral, nor is it purely about efficiency. To go back to containerisation, technology can change the whole ground rules.

Fig. 24 – A Systems-Based Approach to Mapping Out Policies: Eight Criteria

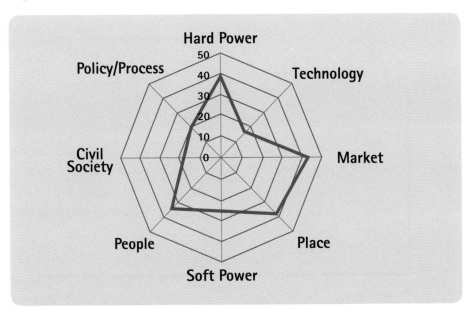

So we are now at a much more complex eight-dimensional frame of public policy. Alas, even at that level, we have oversimplified. Here I want to bring in three other key elements of systems thinking:

A. Path Dependency

To know where we are, we need to know where we came from. There is no 'year zero' in public policy. Understanding why we have what we have is critical.

B. Emergence

Implicit in whatever we have is that it will evolve, often not through the specific intentions of the policy designer, but because of the inherent tendencies in the system that has been evolved. Sometimes this is the result of unintended consequences; sometimes it is the result of people 'gaming' the new system.

C. People (if not policy makers) do not live in silos

Societies are living organisms. As such different parts interact with each other and depend on each other, so no policy operates in a social vacuum.

Fig. 25 – A Systems-Based Approach to Mapping Out Policies: Eight Criteria, and Mapped Out Over Time

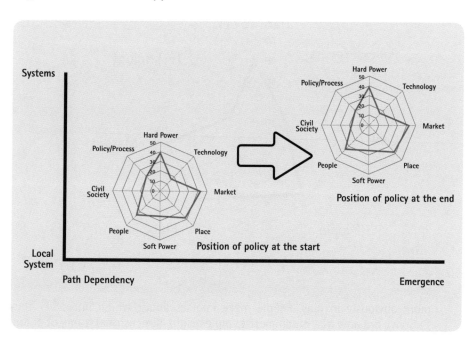

In case this all sounds pretty abstract, let us illustrate it with one universal example of public policy and administration, namely education. So here are the eight dimensions:

1. Hard Power (Realism)

Governments insist that children should be educated. Parents can be fined if they fail their responsibilities. Governments tax people and corporations to finance education, and ban employers from employing children when they should be at school.

2. Soft Power (Normative)

Governments have raised the profile of education. For instance, Jim Callaghan was the first post-war British Prime Minister to make a major speech on school education, since then it would be inconceivable for a Prime Minister to avoid the issue. Tony Blair, of course, famously said his top three priorities were 'Education, education, education.'

3. Civil Society

Whilst Britain was slow to engage volunteers in the classroom, civil society has been key to education. It is not just governors in schools; most of the youth sector is provided within civil society (think scouts, guides etc.); large parts of adult education were also launched within civil society (think of the Workers' Educational Association, etc.).

4. Market

The formal market role in education has been more contentious, with neither academies nor free schools receiving unanimous support. I confess I find this shroud-waving a bit insincere. Even before their introduction, we already had quasi-markets, where the market was in the cost of a house near the best schools. If we go beyond compulsory education, then we see market forces more obviously in play. People make choices about which university they aspire to go to, and which course they aspire to do. No one is advocating a 'No choice' model. We also get illustrations of the perverse effects of this with a massive under-provision of hairdressing courses, and a massive under-subscription for courses such as engineering.

5. Policy/Process

Even within such a specific field as education, each initiative needs to be placed in context, and each initiative affects the eco-system within which it operates. Neither the supporters nor the critics of free schools yet know what their impact will be on the surrounding eco-structure, but both sides expect (differing) outcomes.

6. People

We do not start with *tabula rasa*. People start education with different abilities, different family expectations and support, and different lifestyles. We have always been conscious of class differentials in education. Today, we know that as children progress through school, background often trumps inherent ability in most schools, as many children progress. We also know that family expectations play a significant role. Here in Britain, children of Chinese heritage regularly outperform all other groups, followed by children of Indian heritage. That finding is replicated in the United States. Carolyn Chen, Associate Professor of Sociology at Northwestern, notes that Asian-Americans make up anywhere from '40 to 70 percent of the student population at top public (i.e. state) schools.'[146]

7. Place

A consistent criticism of new education initiatives by education secretaries is that all education is viewed through the prism of a London parent. Yet in many rural areas, the question is not choice of school, it's having a school that stays open.

8. Technology

The impact of technology is evident throughout education, from whiteboards in schools to Massive Online Open Courses (MOOCS) at university level. But the technological impact may be wider, i.e. 'Are our concentration spans getting shorter?' is a question now being asked

If these are our eight dimensions let us also consider our three other drivers

9. Path dependency

Our present provision of schools is located in history. Key milestones were initiatives such as the 1944 Butler Education Act, or the post-war drive

---

[146] Carolyn Chen, 'Asians – Too Smart For Their Own Good?', *New York Times*, December 19, 2012.

towards comprehensive schools (initially championed by Anthony Crosland, though in fact it was during Margaret Thatcher's time as Education Secretary that most comprehensives were created). Similarly, the patchwork quilt of remaining grammar schools reflects specific circumstances and decisions in specific places.

10. Emergence

Systems continuously evolve. We have had over a decade of transfers of powers from Local Education Authorities to schools. Yet we are now witnessing the recreation of clusters – not always geographic – through groupings of academies or federation schools. The education sector remains dynamic, and diverse in shape.

11. Connections to other aspects of society

Though some have tried to keep education to a sole focus, education takes place within a wider context. Education also impacts within that wider context. Let me give three illustrations.

There is much focus on the exponential growth of childhood obesity. Schools are part of that challenge. So we have to address issues such as the quality of school meals, the prevalence of fast food outlets near schools, or the role of P.E. at school. A switch from parents dropping off children on the school run on the drive in to work, to children walking to school, would make an impact.

Secondly, let us consider civics – sometimes seen as an optional extra. However, we now face the challenge of domestic terrorism, and of children being tempted into extremism, so the importance of encouraging shared values takes a much higher priority. The role of education in pre-emptive measures is key.

Thirdly, we need to connect what we teach with what jobs there might be to employ people once they move beyond education.

KISS and CUDDLE

Given the current level of complexity, we can see why simple solutions do not work. We can also see why the tendency to revert to a great structural reorganisation, whilst giving the pretence of change, is normally offered as a substitute for change. Within a systems perspective, I would instead advocate the adoption of that rowing adage, 'Does it make us go faster?' Perhaps the best recent illustration of this has been Dave Beresford's approach with Team Sky cycling. That involved a culture of continuous adaptation. Each adaptation might make only a marginal difference, but collectively they made the team world beaters.

I therefore propose that leaders adopt two maxims **KISS** and **CUDDLE**. Let's take them in turn. Let us suppose I am a year 7 maths teacher – consider some of my challenges. I know what level my pupils should have reached by the end of year 6. I know where I aim to have got them by the end of year 7. But I have to grapple with a wide range of aptitudes and learning. Some will arrive at my class well behind others. My cohort may contain pupils who might be in gifted and talented programmes, and others with special needs. Some may be recent immigrants with very poor English. I have to consider group dynamics; is there a cohort who are disrupting others? Meanwhile, one or two may have very challenging home lives that mean others are taking an interest in the child. So expecting me to also engage in the whole systems thinking seems a step too far. Leaders have a task of trying to **KISS: 'Keep It Simple, Stupid'**, so staff can focus on their day jobs. (That would be my own reworking of part one of the above Kotter 'dual key' idea).

But leaders also need to Embrace **CUDDLE: Compelling storytelling, Unbounded perspective, Dynamics, Devolution, Learning, and Emergence**. With all this fluidity, there is a risk we will adopt a *Que sera sera* attitude. Instead, leaders must embrace:

1. Compelling storytelling

I prefer to talk about 'storytelling', though many of my colleagues prefer to talk about 'public narrative.' Either way, the aim is to develop compelling stories or narratives that motivate, engage and unify staff and citizens. As we have demonstrated in so much of our development work at the Leadership Centre, storytelling / narrative is a skill, but it is a skill that can be learned, and it is a skill that improves with practice. The golfer Gary Player famously summarised this with 'Well, the harder I practice, the luckier I get.'

2. Unbounded perspective

The danger in any organisation is that it becomes introspective. This is particularly the case when the organisation faces unprecedented challenges. Yet any wider understanding of systems thinking requires leaders to look outwards, and to seek connections, otherwise leaders run the risk of being in the 'echo chamber', hearing only internal voices. Leaders need to understand connections, and to move into that space where they can see both what is happening within their organisations, and also where what is happening within wider society. They can then bring different perspectives to bear.

Advocates of 'heroic leadership' might argue that the new role of leaders is to be super-connectors. However, networks transmit viruses at least as effectively as they do ideas. Instead, I would return to the Hefeitz notion of alternating between the balcony and the dance floor. On the dance floor, you are engaging with your particular element of the eco-system. What the balcony allows you to do is to get some sense of how your eco-system fits within the wider picture.

3. Dynamics

In a world of continuous adaptation, standing still effectively means going backwards. Too often, faced with challenges we do not know how to handle, we unconsciously attempt a strategy of 'Stop the world, I want to get off', hoping that we can insulate our activity from what goes on around it. But even if we are successfully engaging with the changing world, then our very success itself affects other parts of the system, thus requiring further change and adaptation on our part.

4. Devolution

Adaptation takes place at the edge. So rather than assuming all change can somehow be centrally driven, we should instead encourage local experimentation. Recognising that change is both difficult and usually also non-linear, we should be more explorative, encouraging continual testing. In software strategies, people often talk of 'fail often, fail fast' (often also adding a third 'fail cheap'.) In other words, there is a recognition that adaptation requires practice. Government sometimes suggests it is adopting this process through pilot programmes. They often fail – but they do not fail fast. Usually, by the time the formal evaluation has taken place, the agenda has already been superseded. A more effective mindset is a presumption of significant experimentation in parallel, which is what devolving achieves.

5. Learning

Another version of the software adage goes 'fail smart, learn fast.' Experimentation only works well if there is a proper feedback loop, so that organisations can be sure that they learn from experimentation. Adaptive organisations have to be learning organisations.

6. Emergence

In the worlds of path dependency and autopoiesis, we need to learn to use the natural momentum whenever appropriate, and otherwise to notice when adaptation is having harmful effects. To go back to the economics illustration I used to discuss systems thinking, Keynes advocated both measures to stimulate confidence, and also warned of the dangers of over-confidence.

There are three other reasons why I like this 'KISS and CUDDLE' formulation. Firstly, it is a phrase in distinct contrast with the more macho language of most 'heroic leadership' books. Secondly, as your husband/wife/partner will tell you, they can tell when you do not really mean it when kissing. Staff know when they are being dumped on. KISS requires leaders to provide some shield for staff, so that they can do their job. Thirdly, when people need a cuddle, they often want some space to ooze out some tension. Given the challenges public service organisations face, the organisational cuddle is the way for leaders to hear and feel those challenges from wider perspectives.

Conclusion

At the core of the argument in this book have been a number of connected propositions.

Firstly, there is a call for us to all act and think more systemically. This does not require completely new abstract theory – it is simply important to remember that to understand a phenomenon means connecting it with other phenomena, through a similarity of patterns. This is particularly the case when we are considering how we interact with other people. We are social animals, we live in communities, we are affected by the society we live in (often in ways we do not appreciate). The idea that we are all isolated individuals each making distinct decisions (the old *homo economicus theory*) is simply wrong.

Secondly, that does not mean we are all alike. Rather, we are all members of different networks, with sometimes different values and presumptions. A presumption therefore that 'one size fits all' is the wrong way to conceive of public services. Instead, I advocate so-called 'clumsy' solutions.

Thirdly, if public services are to be done with citizens rather than done to citizens, we need to be better at engaging with them. Part of that engagement is achieved through storytelling, or public narrative. As I argued extensively in *The Politics of Leadership*, storytelling has a number of functions.[147] There has to be a story (talk the talk); you have to tell the story (walk the talk); you have to be credible (walk the walk); and the story needs to become a shared story (talk the walk). In this book, I have focused on the last of these – the 'public narrative' approach championed by my colleagues is about developing that shared sense of identity that is critical.

Finally, given the sustained financial pressures we face, we need to achieve change at scale, and at pace. Hence I have stressed the importance of better understanding, and of engagement with civil society, but we are also at an exciting point in our understanding of networks and network effects. Here, 'big data' really is a game changer. People like 'Sandy' Pentland and his teams at MIT's Media Lab (and in the many spin-off companies he and his students have created) are showing every day what benefits are possible (as well as some avoidable downsides). In

---

[147] See Joe Simpson, *The Politics of Leadership: A Study of Political Leadership – Politics and Stories* (London: Leadership Centre, 2008).

wanting us to embrace this network approach, let me conclude with two quotes from Viktor Mayer - Schönberger and Kenneth Cukier:

> Today there is an implicit belief among technologists that big data traces its lineage to the silicon revolution. That simply is not so....The IT revolution is evident all around us, but the emphasis has mostly been on the T, the technology. It is time to recast our gaze to focus on the I, the information.[148]

and

> in the spirit of Google and Facebook, the new thinking is that people are the sum of their social relationships, on-line interactions, and connections with content.[149]

It is our challenge as public servants to ensure those insights remain not just in the private sector, but permeate the way we do and see things to help improve the lives of our citizens.

---

[148] Viktor Mayer - Schönberger and Kenneth Cukier, *Big Data: A Revolution That Will Transform How We Live, Work and Think* (London: John Murray, 2013), p. 78.
[149] *Ibid*, p. 157.

Acknowledgements

All works evolve from more than one mind. They are a result of conversations, challenges and learning from others. For the evolution of my thinking, my thanks go especially to all those politicians with whom I have worked over the last thirty or so years. Here at the Leadership Centre, particular thanks should go to my colleagues John Atkinson, Chris Lawrence-Pietroni, Mari Davis, Karen Ellis and David Bolger. Thanks also to the many partners with whom the Leadership Centre has worked, particularly our colleagues on the Systems Leadership Steering Group. This book is an attempt to describe our journey. For turning the argument from outline to book, Seth Thévoz corrected my 'memory' on too many occasions to remember, and the ensured that the book finally emerged with some semblance of sequence.

As ever, all the errors remain mine.

Bibliography

Books

- Paul Addison, *The Road to 1945: British Politics and the Second World War* (London: Jonathan Cape, 1975).

- George A. Akerlof and Robert J. Shiller, *Animal Spirits: How Human Psychology Drives the Economy, and Why It Matters for Global Capitalism* (Princeton: Princeton University Press, 2009).

- George A. Akerlof and Rachel E. Kranton, *Identity Economics: How Our Identities Shape Our Work, Wages and Well-Being* (Princeton, New Jersey: Princeton University Press, 2010).

- Jeffrey C. Alexander, *The Civil Sphere* (Oxford: Oxford University Press, 2006).

- Saul Alinsky, *Rules for Radicals* (New York: Random House, 1971).

- Benedict Anderson, *Imagined Communities: Reflections on the Origin and Spread of Nationalism* (London: Verso, rev. 1991 ed.).

- Aristotle [trans. Carnes Lord], *The Politics* (Chicago, Illinois: Chicago University Press, 1984 [first pub. in Ancient Greek c.350BC).

- W. Brian Arthur, *The Nature of Technology: What It Is, and How It Evolves* (London: Allen Lane, 2009).

- Philip Blond, *Red Tory: How Left and Right Have Broken Britain and How We Can Fix It* (London: Faber & Faber, 2010).

- Jocelyne Bourgon, *A New Synthesis of Public Administration: Serving in the 21st Century* (Ottawa: McGill-Queen's University Press, 2011).

- David Boyle, *Communities Actually: A Study of Liberal Democrat Localism in Action* (London: LGA Liberal Democrats, 2007).

- Edmund Burke, *Reflections on the Revolution in France* (London: SMK Books, 2012 [first pub. 1790]).

- Fritjof Capra, *The Tao of Physics: An Exploration of the Parallels Between Modern Physics and Eastern Mysticism* (Berkeley, California: Shambhala Publications, 1975).

- Fritjof Capra and Pier Luigi Luisi, *The Systems View of Life: A Unifying Vision* (Cambridge: Cambridge University Press, 2014).

- John Charmley, *A History of Conservative Politics Since 1830: Second Edition* (Basingstoke: Palgrave Macmillan, 2008).

- Nicholas A. Christakis and James A. Fowler, Connected: *The Surprising Power of Our Social Networks, and How They Shape Our Lives* (New York: Little, Brown, 2009).

- Peter Clarke, Keynes: *The Rise, Fall, and Return of the 20th Century's Most Important Economist* (London: Bloomsbury, 2009).

- C.A.J. Coady, *Messy Morality: The Challenge of Politics* (Oxford: Oxford University Press, 2008).

- David Colander and Roland Kupers, *Complexity and the Art of Public Policy* (Princeton, New Jersey: Princeton University Press, 2014).

- G.D.H. Cole, *Guild Socialism Re-Stated* (London: Leonard Parsons, 1920).

- John Colville, *The Fringes of Power: Downing Street Diaries, 1939-1955* (London: Wiedenfeld & Nicholson, 1986).

- Cardinal De Richelieu [trans. Jean Desmarets de Saint-Sorlin], *Mirame* (London: Nabu Press, 2012 [first pub. c.1625]).

- Scott Farris, Kennedy and Reagan: *Why Their Legacies Endure* (New York: Lyons Press, 2013).

- David Feldman, *Englishmen and Jews: Social Relations and Political Culture, 1840-1914* (New Haven, Connecticut: Yale University Press, 1994).

- E.M. Forster, *Howard's End* (London: Edward Arnold, 1910).

- John Kenneth Galbraith, *The Great Crash, 1929* (Boston, Massachusetts: Houghton Mifflin, 1954).

- Raymond Geuss, *Philosophy and Real Politics* (Princeton, New Jersey: Princeton University Press, 2008).

- Malcolm Gladwell, *The Tipping Point: How Little Things Can Make a Big Difference* (New York: Little, Brown, 2000).
- Richard S. Grayson, *Belfast Boys: How Unionists and Nationalists Fought and Died Together in the First World War* (London: Continuum, 2009).
- Donald P. Green and Alan S. Gerber, *Get Out the Vote: How to Increase Voter Turnout* (Washington D.C.: Brookings Institution Press, rev. 2008 ed.).
- Graham Greene, *The Third Man: Original Screenplay* (London: Faber and Faber, 1973).
- Peter Hain (ed.), *Community Politics* (London: John Calder, 1976).
- Ronald A. Heifetz, *Leadership Without Easy Answers* (Cambridge, Massachusetts: Harvard University Press, 1994).
- Werner Heisenberg, *Der Teil und das Ganze: Gespräche im Umkreis der Atomphysik* (Munich: R. Piper, 1971).
- Thomas Hobbes, *Leviathan, Parts I and II* (Plymouth: Broadway Press, 2005 [first pub. 1651]).
- Eric Hobsbawm, *The Age of Capital: Europe, 1848-1875* (London: Weidenfeld & Nicholson, 1962).
- Douglas Jay, *The Socialist Case* (London: Faber & Faber 1937).# of Immanuel Kant [Mary Gregor and Jens Timmermann eds.], *Groundwork of the Metaphysics of Morals* (Cambridge: Cambridge University Press, 2012 [first pub. 1785]).
- Daniel Kahneman, *Thinking, Fast and Slow* (New York: Farrar, Straus and Giroux, 2011).
- Arnold Kaufman, 'Human Nature and Participatory Democracy' in William E. Connoly (ed.), *The Bias of Pluralism* (New York: Athlone Press, 1969).
- John Maynard Keynes, *The General Theory of Employment, Interest and Money* (London: Macmillan, 1936).
- Paul Krugman, *The Return of Depression Economics* (London: Penguin, 2008).
- Thomas Kuhn, *The Structure of Scientific Revolutions* (Chicago, Illinois: University of Chicago Press, 1962).
- George Lakoff, *Don't Think of an Elephant: Know Your Values and Frame the Debate* (New York: Chelsea Green, 1990).
- _____, *The Political Mind: Why You Can't Understand 21st-Century Politics with 18th-Century Brain* (New York: Viking, 2008).

- Axel Leijonhufvud, *On Keynesian Economics and the Economics of Keynes* (Oxford: Oxford University Press, 1968).

- Niccolo Macchiavelli, *The Prince* (London: Longman, 2003 [first pub. 1532]).

- Alasdair MacIntyre, *Dependent Rational Animals: Why Human Beings Need Virtues* (Chicago, Illinois: Open Court, 1991).

- Andrew Manis, *Southern Civil Religions in Conflict: Civil Rights and the Culture Wars* (Macon, Georgia: Manis University Press, 2002).

- Sean McMeekin, *The Berlin-Baghdad Express: The Ottoman Empire and Germany's Bid for World Power, 1898-1918* (Cambridge, Massachusetts: Harvard University Press, 2010).

- Steven Ney, *Resolving Messy Policy Problems: Handling Conflict in Environmental, Transport, Health and Ageing Policy* (Abingdon, Earthscan, 2009).

- Mark Moore, *Creating Public Value: Strategic Management in Government* (Cambridge, Massachusetts: Harvard University Press, 1997)

- Joseph S. Nye Jr., *The Powers to Lead* (Oxford: Oxford University Press, 2008).

- Michael Oakeshott, *Rationalism in Politics, and Other Essays* (Indianapolis, Indiana: Liberty Press, 1991).

- Paul Ormerod, *Why Most Things Fail: Evolution, Extinction and Economics* (London: Faber and Faber, 2005).

- _____, *Positive Linking: How Networks Can Revolutionise the World* (London: Faber and Faber, 2012).

- Plato [trans. Benjamin Jowett], *The Republic* (London: Anchor Books, 1980 [first pub. in Ancient Greek, c.380 BC]).

- Alex Pentland, Social Physics: *How Good Ideas Spread – the Lessons From a New Science* (London: Scribe, 2014).

- Karl Popper, *The Poverty of Historicism* (London: Routledge and Kegan Paul, 1961 [rev. ed.]).

- Anthony Powell, *A Dance to the Music of Time*, 12 vols. (London: Fontana, 1957-75, 1975 ed.).

- Robert D. Putnam, *Bowling Alone: The Collapse and Revival of American Community* (New York: Simon & Schuster, 2000).

- John Rawls, *A Theory of Justice* (Cambridge, Massachusetts: Belknap Press, 1971).

- _____, *A Theory of Justice, Second Edition* (Cambridge, Massachusetts: Harvard University Press, 1999).

- Robert Rhodes James, Churchill: *A Study in Failure, 1900-1939* (London: Weidenfeld & Nicholson, 1970).

- Bertrand Russell, *The Good Citizen's Alphabet* (London: Gaberbocchus Press, 1953).

- Amartya Sen, *Identity and Violence: The Illusion of Destiny* (New York: W.W. Norton, 2006).

- Joe Simpson, *The Politics of Place* (London: Leadership Centre, 2006).

- _____, *The Politics of Leadership: A Study of Political Leadership – Politics and Stories* (London: Leadership Centre, 2008).

- Marc Stears, *Demanding Democracy: American Radicals in Search of a New Politics* (Princeton, New Jersey: Princeton University Press, 2010).

- Cass R. Sunstein, On Rumors: *How Falsehoods Spread, Why We Believe Them, What Can Be Done* (New York: Farrar, Straus and Giroux).

- Cass Sunstein and Richard Thaler, *Nudge* (London: Penguin, 2008).

- Michael Szenberg and Lail Ramrattan (eds.), *Eminent Economists II: Their Life and Work Philosophies* (Cambridge: Cambridge University Press, 2014).

- Peter Temin and David Vines, *The Leaderless Economy: Why the World Economic System Fell Apart and How to Fix It* (Princeton, New Jersey: Princeton University Press, 2013).

- Michael Thompson, *Organising and Disorganising: A Dynamic and Non-Linear Theory of Institutional Emergence and its Implications* (Axminster: Triarchy Press, 2008), p. 144.

- Richard Toye, *The Roar of the Lion: The Untold Story of Churchill's World War II Speeches* (Oxford: Oxford University Press, 2013).

- Hugh Trevor-Roper, *The Invention of Scotland: Myth and History* (New Haven, Connecticut: Yale University Press, 2008).

- Robert Venturi, *Complexity and Contradiction in Architecture* (New York: Little, Brown and Co, 1966, rev. 1977 ed.).

- Michael Walzer, *Just and Unjust Wars: A Moral Argument With Historical Illustrations* (New York: Basic Books, 1972 [rev. 2006 ed.]).

- Alexander Watson, *Ring of Steel: Germany and Austria-Hungary at War, 1914-18*

(London: Allen Lane, 2014).

- T.D. Weldon, *The Vocabulary of Politics* (London: Penguin, 1953).
- Orson Welles and Peter Bogdanovich, *This is Orson Welles* (New York: Da Capo Press, 1998 [rev. 2nd ed.]).
- Paul Wilkinson, *Social Movement* (New York City, New York: Praeger, 1971).
- Bernard Williams, 'Politics and Moral Character', in Stuart Hampshire et al. (eds.), *Public and Private Morality* (Cambridge: Cambridge University Press, 1978).

Articles, Essays and Papers

- John Benington and Jean Hartley, Whole Systems Go! *Leadership Across the Whole Public Service System* (Milton Keynes: Open University Business School, 2009).
- Howard Gardner, 'Leadership: A Cognitive Perspective', *SAIS Review*, 16:2 (Summer-Fall 1996), pp.109-22.
- Arthur Downing, 'The Friendly Planet: "Oddfellows", Networks and the "British World", c.1840-1914', *Journal of Global History*, 7:3 (November 2012), pp. 389-414.
- Maurice Glasman, 'Blue Labour and Labour History', Labour History Research Unit, Anglia Ruskin University (October, 2012).
- Peter Hellyer, 'Young Liberals: The "Red Guard" Era', *Journal of Liberal Democrat History*, 17 (Winter 1997-8), pp. 13-5.
- J.R. Hicks, 'Mr. Keynes and the "Classics"', *Econometrica*, 5:2 (Apr 1937), pp. 147-59.
- Samuel P. Huntington, 'The Clash of Civilizations?', *Foreign Affairs*, 72:3 (Summer 1993) pp. 22-49.
- Michael Keeley, 'The Trouble with Transformational Leadership: Toward a Federalist Ethic for Organizations', *Business Ethics Quarterly*, 5:1 (Jan 1995), pp. 71-86.
- Abraham Maslow, 'A Theory of Human Motivation', *Psychological Review*, 50:4 (1943), pp. 370-96.
- James Q. Wilson and George L. Kelling, 'Broken Windows: The Police and Neighborhood Safety', *Atlantic Monthly*, 249:3 (Mar 1982) pp. 29-38.
- Brian Uzzi and Jarrett Spiro, 'Collaboration and Creativity: The Small World Problem', *American Journal of Sociology*, 111:2 (September 2005), pp. 447-504.

Pamphlets

- John Atkinson, David Bolger, Karen Ellis et al, *Total Place: A Practitioner's Guide to Doing Things Differently* (London: Leadership Centre, 2010).

- Bernard Greaves and Gordon Lishman, *The Theory and Practice of Community Politics: ALC Booklet #12* (Hebden Bridge: Association of Liberal Councillors, 1980).

- Michael Meadowcroft, Focus on Freedom: *The Case for the Liberal Party* (Southport: Liberal Party, 1992 [rev. 3rd ed., 2001]).

- Melissa Van Dyke, *Systems Leadership; Exceptional Leadership for Exceptional Times* (London: Colebrook Centre, 2014).

- Richard Vize, *The Revolution Will Be Improvised: Stories and Insights About Transforming Systems* (London: Leadership Centre, 2014).

- Mark Walport (ed.), *Innovation: Managing Risk, Not Avoiding It – Annual Report of the Government Chief Scientific Adviser* (London: Government Office for Science, 2014),

- _____, Innovation: Managing Risk, Not Avoiding It – Evidence and Case Studies (London: Government Office for Sicence, 2014),

Newspapers

- *Daily Telegraph*
- *Guardian*
- *New York Times*
- *New Yorker*
- *The Times*
- *Wall Street Journal*

Lectures and Talks

John Nalbandian, University of Kansas lecture 2006 with credit to John Arnold, CAO, Topeka, Kansas, 'Politics and Administration in Local Government.'

Websites
BBC News, http://news.bbc.co.uk
Durham Constabulary, http://www.durham.police.uk
Margaret Thatcher Foundation, http://www.margaretthatcher.org

Film and Television Series
The Third Man (1949)
The West Wing (1999-2006)

PhD Theses
John Meadowcroft, 'Community Politics: A Study of the Liberal Democrats in Local Government' (Goldsmith's College, University of London, Ph.D., 1999).

Index